HIKE
SEQUIOA AND KINGS CANYON

Hike. Contemplate what makes you happy and what makes you happier still. Follow a trail or blaze a new one. **Hike.** Think about what you can do to expand your life and someone else's. **Hike.** Slow down. Gear up. **Hike.** Connect with friends. Re-connect with nature.

Hike. Shed stress. Feel blessed. **Hike** to remember. **Hike** to forget. **Hike** for recovery. **Hike** for discovery. **Hike.** Enjoy the beauty of providence. **Hike.** Share the way, The Hiker's Way, on the long and winding trail we call life.

HIKE
SEQUOIA AND KINGS CANYON

BY
JOHN MCKINNEY

TheTrailmaster.com

HIKE Sequoia and Kings Canyon By John McKinney

HIKE Sequoia and Kings Canyon © 2022 The Trailmaster, Inc. All rights reserved. Manufactured in the United States of America. No part of this book may be used or reproduced in any manner whatsoever without written permission except in the case of brief quotations embodied in articles and reviews.

Acknowledgments: Many thanks to the Sequoia and Kings Canyon National Park staff, who have been unfailingly courteous and helpful to The Trailmaster in the field. Thanks also for the help on this guide from the office, including Dana M. Dierkes, Branch Chief, Office of Communications & Outreach.

ISBN: 978-0934161-89-3
Book Design by Lisa DeSpain
Cartography by Tom Harrison (TomHarrisonMaps.com)
HIKE Series Editor: Cheri Rae

Published by Olympus Press and The Trailmaster, Inc. www.TheTrailmaster.com (Visit our site for a complete listing of all Trailmaster publications, products, and services.)

Although The Trailmaster, Inc. and the author have made every attempt to ensure that information in this book is accurate, they are not responsible for any loss, damage, injury, or inconvenience that may occur to you while using this information. You are responsible for your own safety; the fact that an activity or trail is described in this book does not mean it will be safe for you. Trail conditions can change from day to day; always check local conditions and know your limitations.

Contents

Introduction 9

Sequoia and Kings Canyon National Parks 15

Sequoia National Park
Giant Forest

Moro Rock 23
   Climb the granite monolith to vistas of the national park and beyond

Round Meadow 27
   Big Trees Trail circles lovely meadow

Beetle Rock 29
   Giant Forest Museum, Beetle Rock history and grand vistas

General Sherman Tree 31
   World's largest living tree and memorable memorial groves

Deeper Into Giant Forest 35
   Trail of the Sequoias offers longer and more tranquil tour of big trees

Twin Lakes 39
   Cahoon Meadow and a pair of inviting lakes

TOKOPAH FALLS 43
    A 1,200-foot beauty, the park's finest falls

HEATHER AND PEAR LAKES 47
    Hike to three lakes on three memorable trails

ALTA MEADOW AND ALTA PEAK 51
    High country destinations with lofty views

MUIR GROVE 55
    Remote grove honors the spirit of the great naturalist

Foothills

MARBLE FALLS 61
    Traipsing along the thunderous Marble Fork of the Kaweah River

PARADISE CREEK 65
    From Hospital Rock to Paradise's swimming pools

Mineral King

MINERAL KING VALLEY 71
    Cold Spring Trail offers easy intro to marvels of Mineral King

MONARCH LAKES AND CRYSTAL LAKES 73
    Two superb sets of high country lakes

EAGLE LAKE 77
    Engaging Eagle Lake, Eccentric Eagle Spring

MOSQUITO LAKES 81
    Glacier scoured valley and five lovely lakes

Giant Sequoia National Monument

BOOLE TREE TRAIL 87
    Visit the largest tree in any of America's national forests

Kings Canyon National Park
Grant Grove

GRANT TREE 93
  World's third-largest tree and onetime showpiece of General Grant National Park

NORTH GROVE 97
  Escape the Grant Grove crowds to a peaceful forest

BIG STUMP BASIN 101
  Way more intriguing than its name suggests

REDWOOD CANYON 103
  Wonderful hiking in the largest sequoia groves on the planet

Cedar Grove

CEDAR GROVE OVERLOOK 109
  Great vistas of length and depth of Kings Canyon

ZUMWALT MEADOWS AND ROARING RIVER FALLS 113
  Saunter over a suspension bridge and along the banks of the Roaring River

MIST FALLS 117
  Stellar pathway along the Kings River with several attractive options

Mount Whitney

MT. WHITNEY 123

SEQUIOA AND KINGS CANYON STORIES 130

ABOUT THE AUTHOR 142

Is that heaven up there or the top of the sequoia?

EVERY TRAIL TELLS A STORY.

INTRODUCTION

Come for the sequoia, stay for the Sierra.

And take a hike.

If you only drive through you'll be disappointed: Sequoia and Kings Canyon have the superlative scenery and postcard views found in the country's most noted national parks, but you have to hike to find them.

Naturally the groves of sequoia are the primary draw to both namesake Sequoia National Park and to Kings Canyon National Park. "Noblest of a noble race," is how the great naturalist John Muir described the trees, biggest on earth, and the prime reason for the formation of the parks. General Sherman, standing 274 feet tall and measuring 36.5 feet in diameter at the base of its massive trunk, is the largest of the large trees.

Scenic 46-mile-long Generals Highway connects the national parks and offers access to the most popular sequoia groves, but auto travel is restricted to lower and middle elevations, so if you want to fully experience the park you need to hike into the Sierra Nevada high country.

Want to get away from it all? Famed High Sierra Trail extends east-west across Sequoia National Park. Nearly half of one of the great trails of the world—the 225-mile long John Muir Trail—extends through Sequoia and Kings Canyon national parks. By some accounts, a backpacker in Sequoia National Park can hike to a spot farther away from roads than anywhere else in the continental U.S.

Long-distance backpacking expeditions aren't required to reach many of the alpine charms of Sequoia and Kings Canyon national parks. Where the road ends, an extensive trail system begins and many of the parks' most compelling natural attractions—waterfalls, rivers, lakes, vista points and remote sequoia groves—can be reached by easy, moderate and all-day hikes.

HIKE Sequoia and Kings Canyon collects my favorite day hikes in what the National Park Service considers to be the five major regions of the parks: Giant Forest, Mineral King and the Foothills areas of Sequoia National Park plus the Grant Grove and Cedar Grove areas of Kings Canyon National Park.

As a bonus I've added a hike in adjacent Giant Sequoia National Monument, a haven for the big trees administered by the U.S. Forest Service.

The groves are great, but it's possible to take many hikes in Sequoia and Kings Canyon national parks without sighting a single sequoia. Hillsides with

Introduction

chaparral and dotted with oaks aren't exactly rare in California but the California Foothills ecosystem in the lower elevations around Ash Mountain in Sequoia National Park is the only one in the nation under National Park Service protection. Some foothill trails, including footpaths along forks of the Kaweah River, can be hiked all year around.

Mineral King, a gorgeous, avalanche-scoured valley ringed by rugged 12,000-foot peaks, is another area irresistible to hikers. Views from atop the Great Western Divide and the many lakes hidden in glacial cirques compel hikers to return summer after summer.

The hiking season for much of Sequoia and Kings Canyon national parks is a fairly short one. Middle

Mineral King: Land of lakes and classic Sierra peaks.

elevations—5,000 to 9,000 feet—are often snow-covered from November through May. In Mineral King, and higher in the High Sierra, the season can be even shorter.

If you have only one day (promise yourself to return soon when you have more time!), drive from Grant Grove to Giant Forest or vice-versa and hike amidst the magnificent sequoia in each locale.

Ideally, the hiker needs at least three days to get a fair sampling of Sequoia and Kings Canyon National Parks. Take in the sequoia groves on the first day, on the second day, head for the high country (Lakes Trail is a good choice) and on the third day, take a hike in Mineral King.

I've selected the best hikes for a variety of scenery and for a range of abilities: memorable family walks among the big trees, pleasant excursions to lakes and waterfalls, and some challenging hikes high into the Sierra Nevada.

More than one million visitors per year pass through the parks, and major trails are well-traveled during the summer, but I've rarely felt overwhelmed by humanity when hiking in Sequoia and Kings Canyon national parks. Many hikers have told me they have found quiet and tranquility on the trail to the park's natural treasures—provided, of course, you avoid tourist-trafficked hot spots such as Moro Rock and General Sherman Tree.

Introduction

When I hit the trail in Sequoia and Kings Canyon national parks, I feel as if I'm living large and hiking larger: the trees are huge, the mountains high, the canyons deep and the trail system is quite extensive—a well-maintained network of more than 800 miles. The parks offer hundreds of thousands of acres of untouched Sierra high country, of which more than 90 percent is designated wilderness. If you're a hiker, that's a dream come true.

Hike smart, reconnect with nature and have a wonderful time on the trail.

Hike on.

—John McKinney

Mt. Whitney and other high peaks along the Sierra crest were added to Sequoia National Park in 1926.

EVERY TRAIL TELLS A STORY.

Sequoia and Kings Canyon National Parks

Geography

Sequoia and Kings Canyon national parks are located in the southern Sierra Nevada, by some accounts the largest mountain range in the U.S. The parks boast a remarkable range of elevations from 1,600 feet to more than 14,000 feet, and a range of ecologies from Mediterranean to alpine. Kings Canyon is one of the continent's deepest canyons (2,000 feet deeper than Grand Canyon) and 14,494-foot Mt. Whitney is the highest peak in the continental U.S.

Measuring 66 miles long and 36 miles wide at their widest point, the two contiguous parks have only two road entrances. Highway 198 east, via Visalia and the town of Three Rivers, leads to the Ash Mountain Entrance in Sequoia National Park, and Highway 180 east, via Fresno, leads straight to the Big Stump Entrance near Grant Grove in Kings Canyon National Park. Both entrances are approximately 4 hours from Los Angeles and 5 hours from San Francisco.

History

In the 1860s, people came to saw the big trees, not see them. Grove upon grove of giant sequoias were toppled and milled into lumber. John Muir's nature writing and newspaperman George Stewart, editor of the *Visalia Delta*, marshaled public opinion to form Sequoia and General Grant national parks.

These national parks, which now boast such big attractions, started out rather small. Sequoia, the nation's second national park, totaled 50,000 acres when it was established in 1890. General Grant National Park, forerunner of Kings Canyon, was established a week after Sequoia and initially included only 2,560 acres.

The U.S. Cavalry patrolled General Grant National Park after it was established in 1890.

Mt. Whitney and adjacent high country was added to Sequoia National Park in 1926. Mineral King's valley, peaks, and alpine lakes became part of the park in 1978 after a lengthy battle between ski resort developers and conservationists led by the Sierra Club.

A greatly expanded Kings Canyon National Park, incorporating the old General Grant National Park, was established in 1940.

Natural History

Lower park elevations include chaparral-cloaked slopes and oak woodland. At higher elevations (5,000 to 9,000 feet) the landscape is

The Three Bears—and their Mom. Bears roam the backcountry and sometimes venture into populated parts of the parks.

dominated by conifer forest—the giant sequoias along with Ponderosa, Jeffrey, sugar and lodgepole pines and white and red fir. Lush meadows are watered by abundant creeks.

Visitors often see squirrels and mule deer as well as the occasional black bear. Groundhog Meadow in Mineral King is named for the abundant furry marmots—relatives of East Coast woodchucks.

The sequoias, reduced in number over millions of years by ecological and climatic changes, and further reduced by logging, survive today only in isolated groves on the Sierra Nevada's western slope. Thirty of the world's 75 groves, as well as the largest individual trees, are found in the national parks.

Sequoias are survivors. Some live 3,000 years or more, and many mature park specimens are 1,500 years old. It's very thick bark (up to 2 feet) resists insects, disease and fire.

By far the greatest threat to the sequoia's survival as a species is climate change, as evidenced by increasingly frequent and intense wildfires. The eyes of the world were on the sequoias in August 2020 when the raging Castle Fire advanced on the groves. We watched the intense blaze attack the vulnerable crowns of the giant sequoias and destroy thousands of them. General Sherman Tree, wrapped in foil, was spared, but some 7,500 to 10,600 mature giant sequoias were lost, about 10 to 14 percent of the world's population.

Iconic General Sherman Tree, wrapped in foil to protect it from raging wildfires.

Clearly, we need an urgent response to the climate crisis that includes stepped-up forest management. The sequoias—and we humans—are in a new reality and the sooner we act the better.

Administration

Sequoia and Kings Canyon national parks share a boundary and are administered as one park by the National Park Service. Check out the National Park Service website at nps.gov/seki for the most up-to-date information on the park, lodging, hikes, regulations, and the best times to visit. Information plus road conditions are available by phone (559-565-3341). You can also get a variety of books and maps from the Sequoia Natural History Association (sequoiahistory.org; 559-565-3759).

EVERY TRAIL TELLS A STORY.

I
Sequoia National Park

HIKE ON.

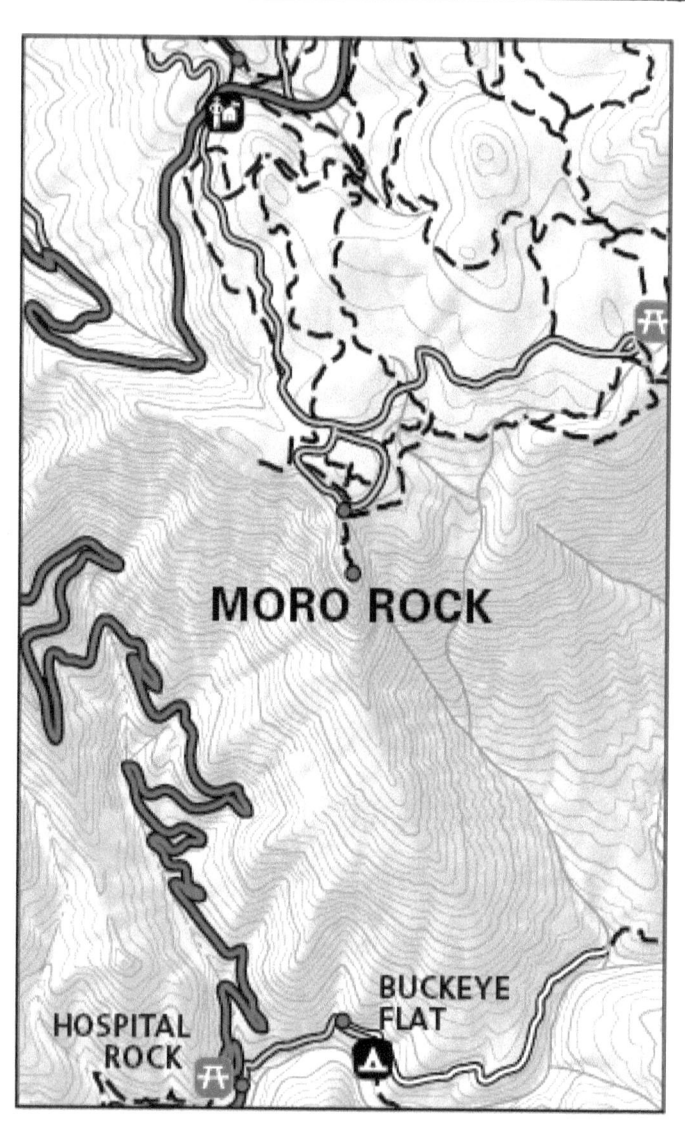

TheTrailmaster.com

Moro Rock

Moro Rock Trail

0.6 mile round trip with 300-foot elevation gain

The top of Moro Rock is by far Sequoia's most popular vista point. "I climbed Moro Rock" T-shirts have been souvenirs for decades and the short hike is still one of Sequoia's best known and most popular.

The view from on high is one reason for the rock's fame and acclaim. From the 6,725-foot granite summit, located in the center of the park, the hiker savors magnificent vistas of the Middle Fork of the Kaweah River, located some 4,000 feet below.

The panorama includes the Great Western Divide and its near-14,000-footers, and one-third or so of Sequoia National Park, including Generals Highway and the Middle and Marble forks of the Kaweah River. On especially clear days, view the San Joaquin Valley and glimpse the Coast Range on the distant horizon, more than 100 miles away.

The trail itself—more of stairway, really—is a stunning example of the trail builder's art (circa 1931) and another reason for Moro Rock's popularity as a sight-to-see. Park service interpretation at the trailhead detail how the path was hewn from the granite. One wonders how early park visitors braved the rock without ramps and railings.

In 1917, a wooden stairway was built and deteriorated rapidly. Its 1931 replacement, a 797-foot-long stairway attempted to use natural surfaces as much as possible and to follow the natural contours of Moro Rock. The stairway is on the National Register of Historic Places.

Perhaps such improvements, along with generations of publicity, have made Moro Rock a bit too popular because summer auto traffic around the rock is dispiriting to say the least. Park planners have considered closing the access road to autos and making it accessible only to hikers and shuttle buses.

Hikers can at least avoid the trailhead jam by hiking to Moro Rock (a 3-mile walk or so) from the central Giant Forest area. An early start, a sunset hike, or an autumn excursion can also help beat the crowds.

This is also a good trailhead to access via the park's shuttle bus system. From late May to early September, board a bus from nearby Giant Forest Village or from shuttle stops farther away.

Anyway, this is a must-do hike. While you can find peace and even a little solitude in multiple sequoia groves, there really is only one Moro Rock.

DIRECTIONS: From Generals Highway by the Giant Forest Museum, follow Crescent Meadow Road 1.2 miles and turn right onto the one-way road looping through Moro Rock parking area.

THE HIKE: Start marching up the trail—a series of switchbacks, rock ramps and 353 granite steps. No need to wait for the top to start enjoying those grand views because they unfold as you ascend, but the summit panorama is the most glorious of all. The railing-enclosed top of the rock has an excellent summit-locator to help you ID the many peaks and features visible from this amazing vantage point.

On a clear day (sadly, increasingly rare), you can see forever from Moro Rock.

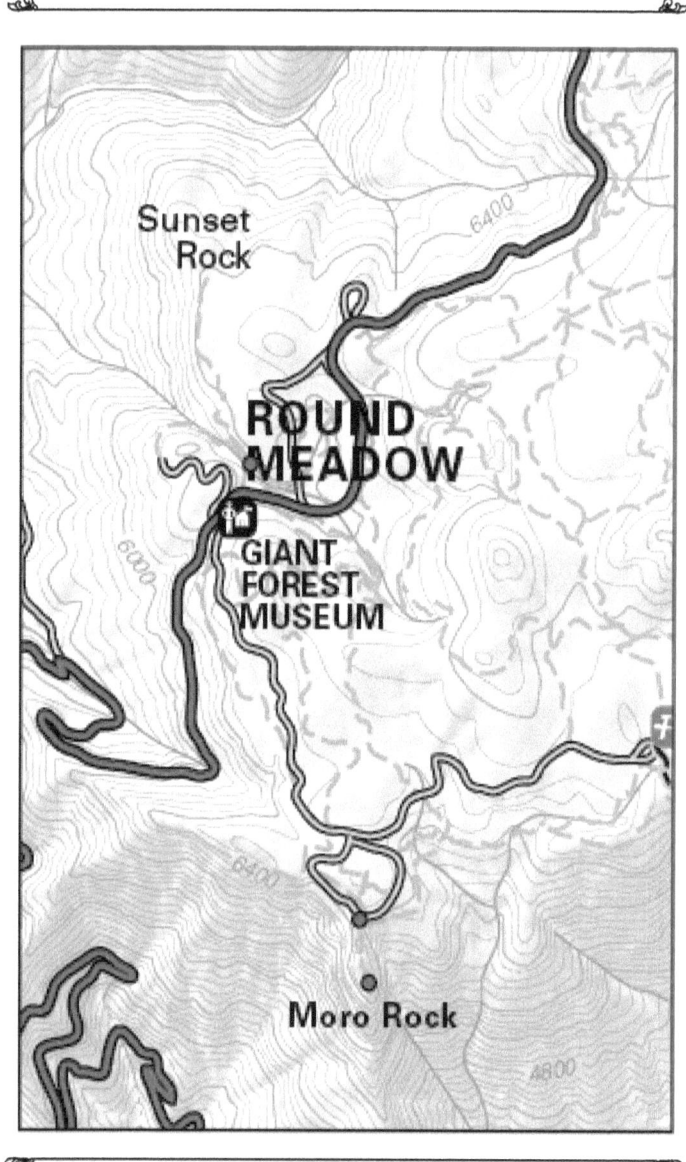

TheTrailmaster.com

Round Meadow

Big Trees Trail

1.2-mile loop around Round Meadow

Big Trees Trail, a full-access asphalt pathway, loops around Round Meadow and interprets sequoia ecology. The sequoia look particularly gigantic when viewed from across the meadow. The Giant Forest Museum features intriguing interactive exhibits and serves as hub for a number of nature trails. (See Beetle Rock hike description.)

DIRECTIONS: Giant Forest Museum is about a one-hour drive up Generals Highway from the Ash Mountain entrance. The signed trail is next to the museum.

THE HIKE: Interpretive Signs tell the story of the sequoia, young and old, and point out some fine specimens, including Clara Barton Tree, named for the founder of the American Red Cross. In late spring, wildflowers dot Round Meadow.

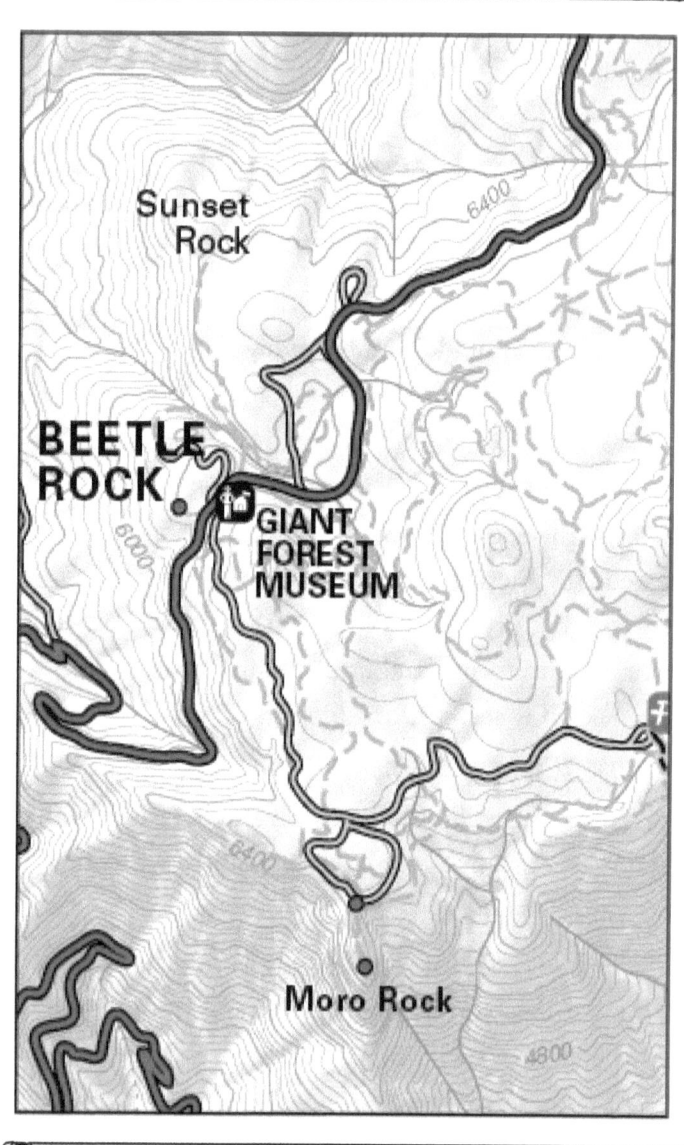

TheTrailmaster.com

Beetle Rock

Beetle Rock Trail

From Giant Forest Museum to Beetle Rock is 0.5 mile round trip

Author Sally Carrighar roamed the rock in the 1940s and penned *One Day at Beetle Rock*, a lively account of nine animals spending a day on the large expanse of granite. Kids love scrambling across Beetle Rock and adults love the views.

DIRECTIONS: Giant Forest Museum is about a one-hour drive up Generals Highway from the Ash Mountain entrance.

THE HIKE: From the south side of the museum parking lot, walk the short park road to Beetle Rock Education Center.

Clear-day vistas from Beetle Rock can include the Sierra foothills, Central Valley and even the coast range, 100 miles away. Beetle Rock Trail continues to meet a road between giant, Giant Forest parking lots.

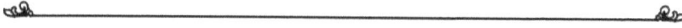

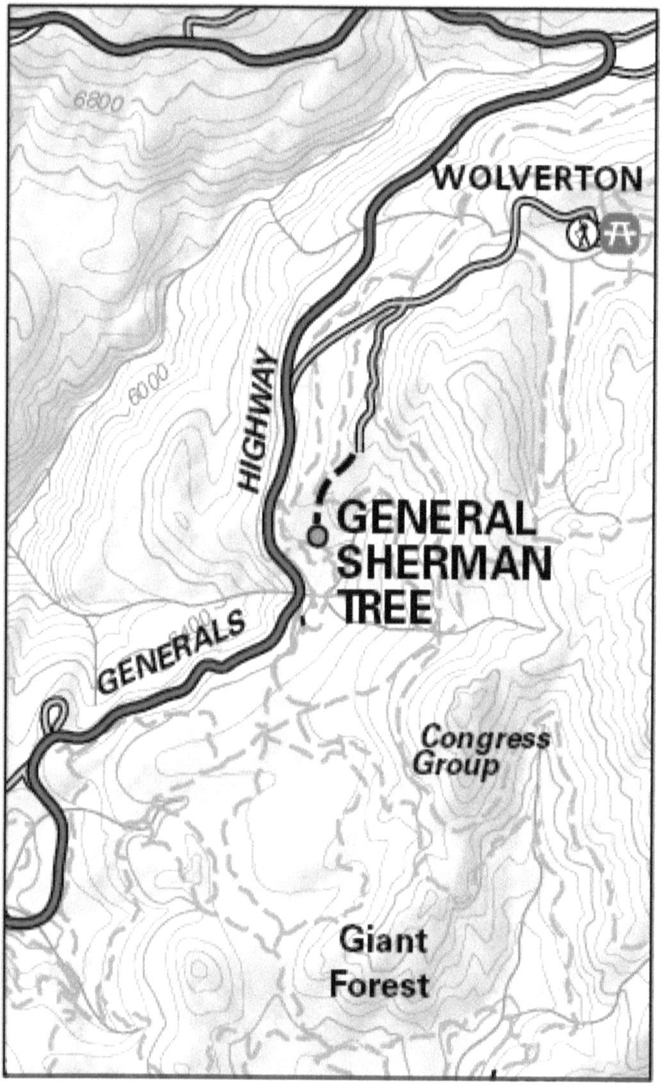
6800
WOLVERTON
6000
HIGHWAY
GENERAL
SHERMAN
TREE
GENERALS
Congress
Group
Giant
Forest

GENERAL SHERMAN TREE

CONGRESS TRAIL

To General Sherman Tree is 0.6 mile round trip; to The Senate Grove is 2-mile loop

Sure it's a tourist attraction, reached by the masses via a paved trail, but no visit to Sequoia National Park is complete without a look at the General Sherman Tree, the world's largest living tree.

The tree's vital statistics: 275 feet high, between 2,300 to 2,700 years old. General Sherman is some 52,500 cubic feet in volume and weighs an estimated 2.8 million pounds.

The tree was originally named for Civil War General William Sherman, then renamed Karl Marx Tree for a time by the Kaweah Colonists, who founded what they hoped would be a socialist utopia here in the forest.

Continue your tour of the magnificent sequoia on Congress Trail, which visits groups of trees named for the House and Senate, as well as trees named for presidents and assorted famous individuals. It's an interpreted nature trail that loops through the Giant Forest where four of the five largest trees dwell. Despite the crowds, the park's most popular path is an enjoyable and educational walk for the whole family.

DIRECTIONS: From Generals Highway, turn west on Wolverton Road and drive a half mile. Turn right for "Sherman Tree" and proceed 0.8 mile to the large parking lot.

THE HIKE: Head down the paved path with many stairs and likely with lots of company 0.3 mile to pay your respects to the General Sherman Tree.

Next, be thankful for what you don't see. Most buildings were removed from Giant Forest, part of a decade-long National Park Service project. Tourist facilities and services were relocated a few miles north to Wuksachi Village.

From the trailhead close to Sherman Tree, join signed and paved Congress Trail. Cross Sherman Creek on a wooden bridge and begin your tour of the giant sequoias, including aptly named Leaning Tree and some fire-scarred old veterans.

Ancient the trees are, but they're not frozen in time and they display their individuality: some lightning-struck Sequoias have lost their crowns, others have been blackened by fire. Some long-dead specimens still stand.

The National Park Service has made a couple of major changes in its Giant Forest management policy. After many decades of fire suppression efforts, the agency has instituted a program of controlled burns designed to improve the forest's health, and to reduce the risk by removing accumulated brush and thinning vegetation. (It's a bit disconcerting to some visitors when they see blackened tree trunks and don't realize that fire is a necessary element of forest ecology.)

About a mile out, pass a junction with Alta Trail and soon reach an inspiring group known as The Senate. A short descent along the fern-filled forest path leads to The House, another wondrous group. The path visits McKinley Tree and continues a final 0.5-mile back to Sherman Tree. Head up the walkway and stairs back to the parking lot.

General Sherman, the world's largest living tree.

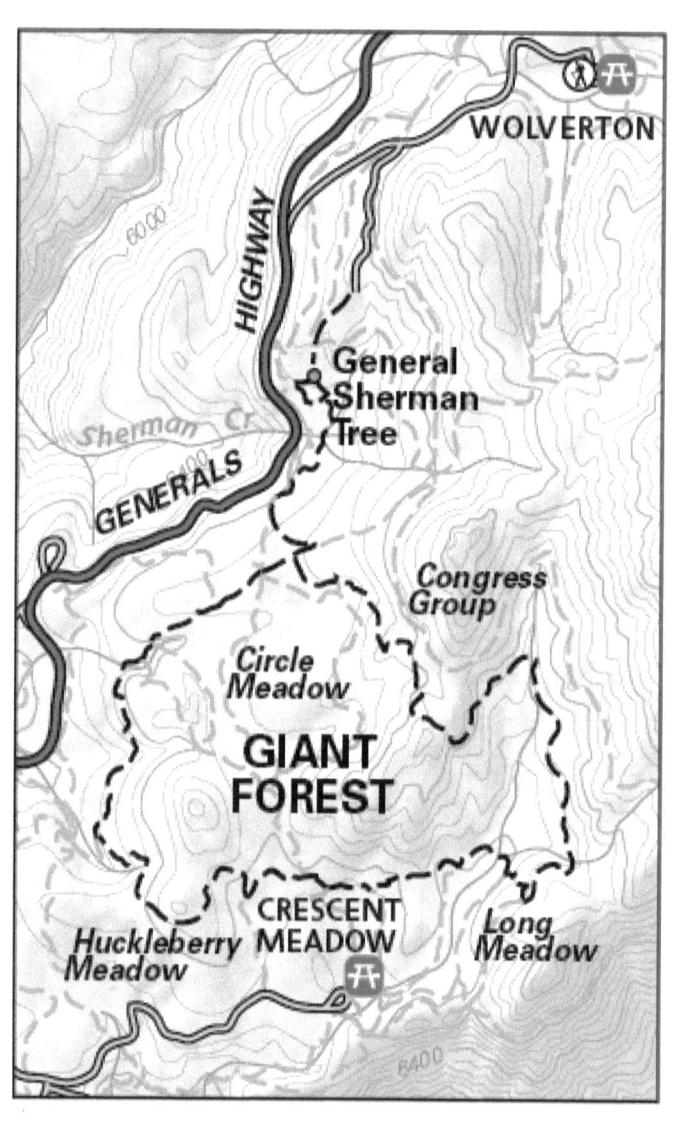

Deeper into Giant Forest

Congress Trail, Trail of the Sequoias

Congress Trail is 2-mile loop; Trail of the Sequoias is 5.1-mile loop with 500-foot elevation gain

Many are the wonders of the John Muir-named Giant Forest, which holds the park's greatest concentration of sequoias—more than 8,000 big trees. Begin by joining visitors from across the country and around the world on the short walk to General Sherman Tree, the world's largest living thing. Next meander Congress Trail, is an interpreted nature trail that loops through the Giant Forest where four of the five largest trees dwell.

Trail of the Sequoias is for the hiker looking for more—more Giant Forest, more hiking, and a little more tranquility. It's not exactly off-the-beaten path, but it is a much-less traveled route.

DIRECTIONS: From Generals Highway, turn west on Wolverton Road and drive a half mile. Turn right for "Sherman Tree" and proceed 0.8 mile to the large parking lot.

THE HIKE: Head down the paved path with many stairs and likely with lots of company 0.3 mile to pay your respects to the General Sherman Tree. The tree's vital statistics: 275 feet high, 102 feet in circumference, between 2,300 to 2,700 years old. General Sherman is some 52,500 cubic feet in volume and weighs an estimated 2.8 million pounds.

From the trailhead close to Sherman Tree, join signed and paved Congress Trail. Cross Sherman Creek on a wooden bridge and begin your tour of the giant sequoias, including aptly named Leaning Tree and some fire-scarred old veterans.

Hikers from near and far wonder why so many magnificent trees in Sequoia National Park are stuck with the names of politicos and obscure presidents. The Washington Tree, named for America's revered first president, seems appropriate. But the McKinley Tree? The Cleveland Tree?

Don't look for the Bill Clinton Tree, George Bush Tree or Barack Obama Tree anytime soon; the national park service abandoned the practice of naming big trees after World War II.

Paved Congress Trail leads a short mile to a junction with Trail of the Sequoias. Join this path for a half-mile ascent to this hike's high point, then descend gradually 1.5 miles among more sequoias to Long Meadow.

At the upper end of this meadow is Tharps Log, a cabin used for 30 summers until 1890 by cattle rancher Hale Tharp. From the cabin, you'll join Crescent Meadows Trail, passing the severely scarred, but still standing Chimney Tree.

Four miles out, join Huckleberry Trail for a brief climb, then follow signs to Circle Meadow, very shortly arriving at another trail junction. Trail of the Sequoias forks right (northeast), traveling a mile to the Senate Group and rejoining Congress Trail for the return to the General Sherman Tree trailhead.

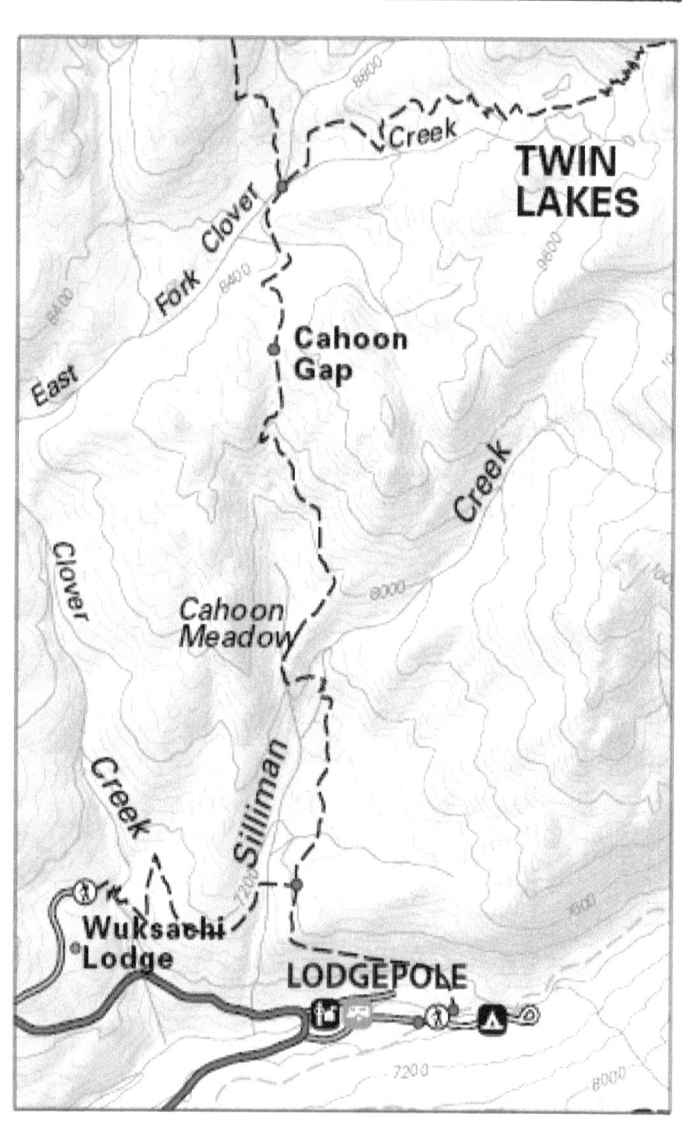

TWIN LAKES

TWIN LAKES TRAIL

To Cahoon Meadow is 5.2 miles round trip with 1,000-foot elevation gain; to Clover Creek Trail Camp is 10 miles round trip with 2,000-foot gain; to Twin Lakes is 13.6 miles round trip with 2,800-foot gain

Beginning near the Tokopah Falls trailhead, the hike to Twin Lakes is a classic High Sierra hike, complete with mixed conifer forest, frisky creeks, flowery meadows and a heart-pounding climb to two popular lakes.

Some veteran Sierra hikers find Pear Lake a bit too populated for their tastes and take the trail to Twin Lakes instead, though it must be said, Twin Lakes Trail is well-traveled, too.

Twin Lakes, perched in a basin below Silliman Crest, are not a matched set, but do offer an inviting destination. The smaller twin is fringed with marshy meadow, the larger lake's shoreline is a combination of forest and big boulders.

The journey to Twin Lakes is a moderate backpacking trip and a rather strenuous day hike. If you're not quite up for the all-day jaunt to Twin Lakes and back, Clover Creek Camp, 5 miles out, beckons with good fishing and fine picnic areas.

I like beginning the hike to Twin Lakes on the 1.5-mile long Wuksachi Trail, which begins past the center of Wuksachi Village at the far end of the last parking lot. The path (popular with hotel guests but usually lightly used) travels amidst fir forest and soon switchbacks down to a bridge across Clover Creek. Then it's up forested slopes to another bridge, this one over Silliman Creek. The mellow path junctions Twin Lakes Trail about 1.6 miles from the trailhead at Lodgepole.

DIRECTIONS: At the east end of Lodgepole, at Log Bridge over the Marble Fork of the Kaweah River, park in the hikers lot on the south side of the river. Cross the bridge on foot to the signed trailhead, located a short distance past the Tokopah Falls trailhead.

THE HIKE: Skirt Lodgepole Campground, then ascend briskly west up wooded slopes, then north above Silliman Creek. Climbing through a thick forest of lodgepole pine and fir, you pass a junction with Wuksachi Trail 1.6 miles from the trailhead, cross Silliman Creek at the 2.2-mile mark, and reach the campsites at lush Cahoon Meadow after another 0.4

mile of travel. Deer often browse the tall grass of the meadow.

Another 1.8 miles of climbing leads to fir-forested Cahoon Gap at the 4.2-mile mark. The path then descends 0.8 mile to Clover Creek Camp.

Leveling out, the trail follows Clover Creek Valley to a junction with JO Pass Trail at 5.5 miles. Keep right and begin another climb through thinning forest, along the Twin Lakes outlet creek, and over granite slopes. The path deposits you on the north shore of the larger lake. Take a short spur trail leftward to the smaller of the Twin Lakes. On a warm summer day, take a refreshing swim in the shallow lakes before hiking back the way you came.

The journey to—and beyond—Twin Lakes is a classic High Sierra hike.

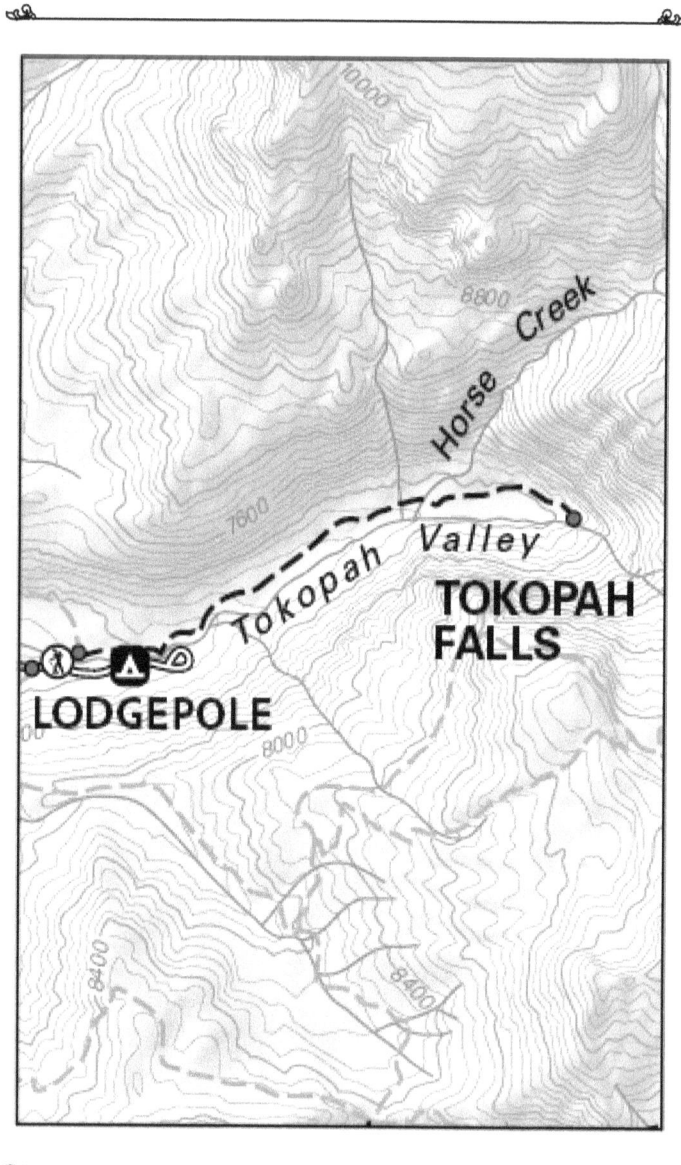

TOKOPAH FALLS

TOKOPAH VALLEY TRAIL

3.4 miles round trip with 500 foot elevation gain

Lodgepole Campground, Sequoia National Park's major recreation hub, rests at the bottom of a dramatic canyon cut by the Marble Fork of the Kaweah River. For the hiker, this hub's canyon bottom location means it's all uphill from here.

Tokopah is said to be a native Yokut word meaning "high mountain valley." Not high enough, you might think as you stand in the 6,700-foot high valley, gaze way up at the surrounding backcountry and think of the ascent required to reach it.

Happily for the casual hiker, a fairly mellow trail parallels the Marble Fork and leads to 1,200-foot high Tokopah Falls, often regarded as the finest in Sequoia and Kings Canyon National Parks. Most vigorous in the spring when windblown spray can soak you as you approach, the falls cascade over the dramatic granite cliffs.

The mostly-level path, suitable for kids and families, meanders amidst tall pines, crosses a couple of creeks on bridges, then voila!—a clear view of the falls. Kids might also get a kick out of viewing the bold and furry marmots known to roam around the area at the base of the falls.

While picturesque, and the tallest waterfall in Sequoia National Park, Tokopah does not seem that high to this hiker—not from afar and not from the base of the falls. Appearance is reality, I suppose, and because Tokopah is a series of cascades rather than one of those famed one-big-free-fall waterfalls in Yosemite, you tend to doubt its measurements.

Equally inspiring is the hike to the falls which offers close-up views of the Marble Fork, a glacially carved tributary of the Kaweah River, and the magnificent Watchtower looming above Tokopah Valley. Other highlights include the polished granite canyon walls, the boulder-strewn river bed and a mixed forest of lodgepole pine, fir and incense cedar.

This is a popular hike, particularly with campers staying at Lodgepole Campground. Hit the trail early if it's solitude you crave.

DIRECTIONS: Begin at Lodgepole's east end by Log Bridge over the Marble Fork of the Kaweah River. The trail begins just north of the bridge. Parking is on the south side of the river.

THE HIKE: Follow the woodsy trail along the Kaweah River, emerging from the forest in 0.5 mile to get a pretty good view of the Tokopah Valley. Cross a meadow (stay on trail) and a bit more than a mile out, cross Horse Creek on a wooden footbridge.

As you near the falls, traverse boulder-strewn terrain on a well-engineered length of trail, then lift your eyes to behold Tokopah Falls. The impressive path, which was dynamited right into the granite, leads right to the edge of the falls.

(Please don't scramble up the steep and slick rocks in order to see more of the upper falls. You could slip and die.)

Many hikers regard Tokopah as the finest falls in the national parks.

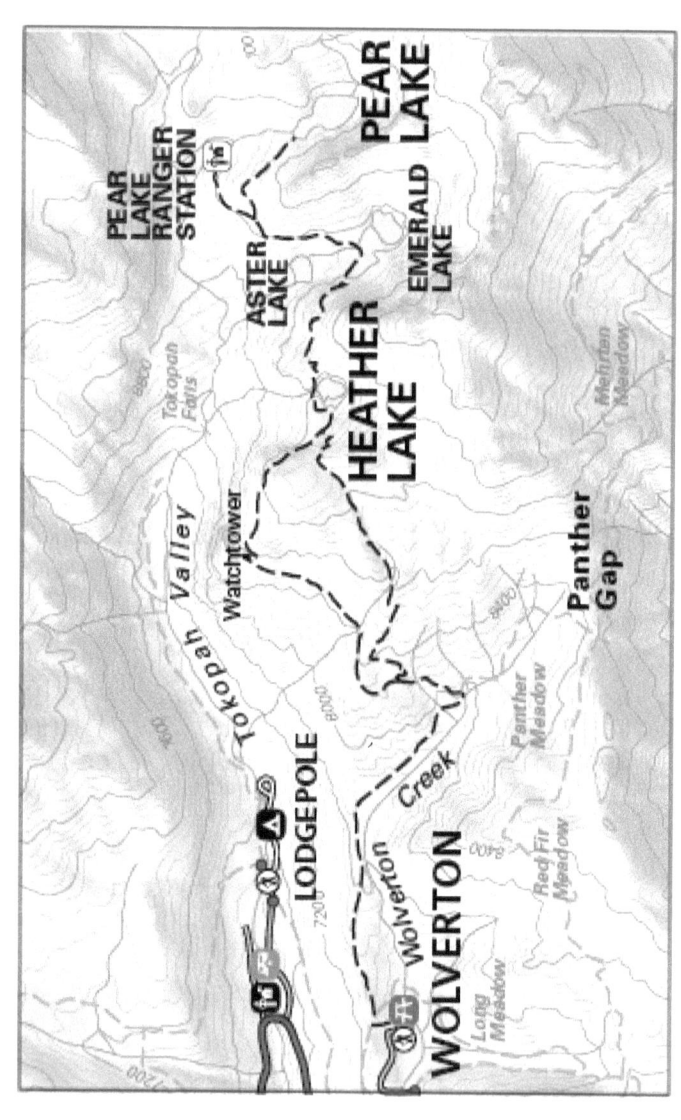

TheTrailmaster.com

Heather & Pear Lakes

Lakes, Watchtower, Hump Trails

From Wolverton to Heather Lake is 8.4 miles round trip; to Emerald Lake is 10.5 miles round trip; to Pear Lake is 12.5 miles round trip with 2,200-foot elevation gain

Lakes Trail delivers the promise in its name: Heather, Emerald, Aster and Pear lakes. Many hikers consider it the best backcountry hike in Sequoia National Park.

The little lakes called tarns rest in rock bowls scoured by glaciers long ago. Named for the red heather growing nearby, Heather Lake, first along the way, is a fine destination. With an early start, the ambitious hiker can visit all four lakes in a day.

This hike also boasts two awesome trails. Watchtower Trail, dynamited out of rock by the Civilian Conservation Corps back in the 1930s, is a stunning example of the trail builder's art. The path leads along the edge of a dramatic and precipitous rock formation and is dangerous when icy or covered with snow.

(A less nerve-wracking alternative is Hump Trail, rising every bit as steeply as its name suggests.)

DIRECTIONS: From Generals Highway, three miles north of Giant Forest Village, take the Wolverton turnoff and proceed 1.5 miles to a large parking area and signed Lakes Trail.

THE HIKE: Climb concrete steps to an information board, trailhead and signed Lakes Trail. In just 0.1 mile, meet a path leading to the Lodgepole area of the park. Keep on Lakes Trail and ascend a ridge amidst red fir forest.

A mile out, the trail ascends above Wolverton Creek and passes a lovely meadow. Curving southeast, the path meets signed Panther Gap Trail 1.75 miles from the trailhead and in another 0.25 mile a junction with Watchtower and Hump trails.

Both trails lead to Heather Lake and beyond. Watchtower Trail ascends moderately at first to a meadow, then more steeply with switchbacks up to The Watchtower, climbing onto a granite ledge. Next the dizzying path traces the cliff-face, far, far, above Tokopah Valley. Great views if you dare take your eyes off the trail, which rejoins Hump Trail in another 0.75 mile.

Hump Trail: Begin a 1.25 mile grind, gaining more than 1,000 feet in elevation in the first mile, ascending through red fir forest to a more rocky

Heather & Pear Lakes

landscape. At the top of the hump, enjoy the views and switchback down to meet Watchtower Trail.

From the Watchtower-Hump Trail reunion, travel a mellow 0.25 mile to tranquil Heather Lake. Next the trail ascends and descends a foxtail pine-spiked ridge 1.25 miles to Emerald Lake. Like Heather, Emerald Lake is situated at about 9,200 feet in elevation.

(Follow Emerald Lake's outlet creek downhill 0.2 mile to reach little Aster Lake.)

Lakes Trail turns north and climbs another ridge, this one separating Emerald Lake from Pear Lake, and continues to a junction. A 0.25-mile-long side trail leads to Pear Lake Ranger Station (staffed in summer).

Stay with the right fork and ascend a short 0.5 mile to Pear Lake, largest lake en route. Check out what might be the most stunningly situated solar toilet in all of the High Sierra.

Lakes, Watchtower and Hump trails add up to a hike you'll long remember.

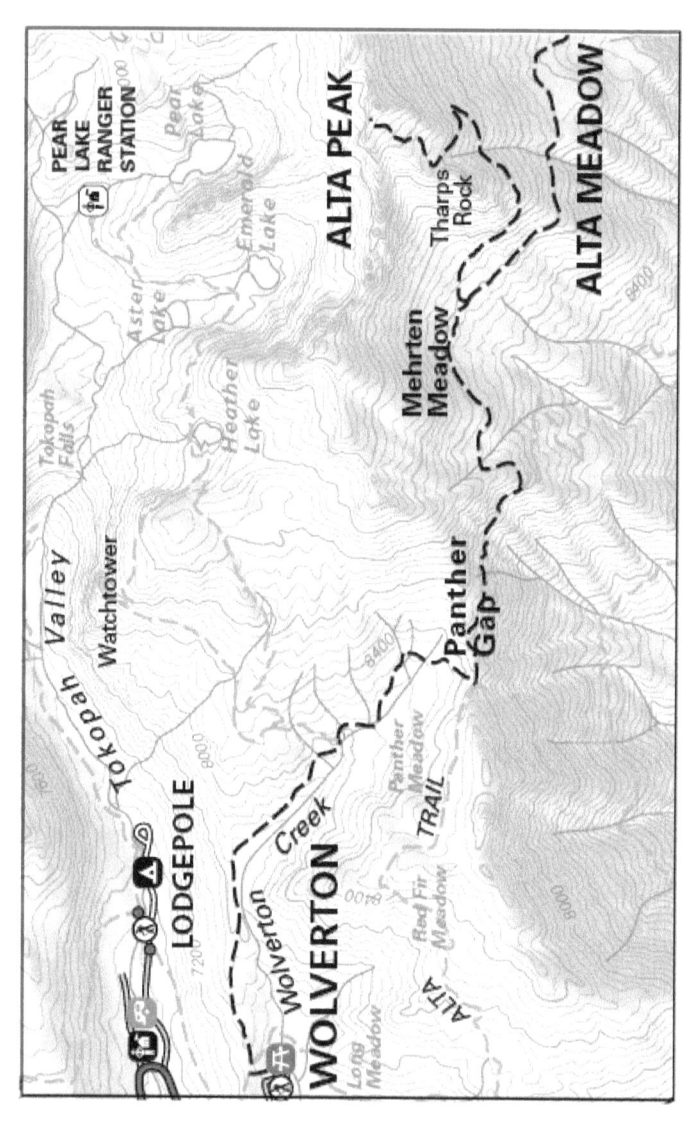

Alta Meadow & Alta Peak

Lakes, Panther Gap, Alta Trails

To Panther Gap is 5.5 miles round trip with 1,100-foot elevation gain; to Alta Meadow is 11.5 miles round trip with 2,000-foot elevation gain; to Alta Peak is 13.75 miles with 3,900-foot elevation gain

Alta Peak and mighty Mt. Whitney are the only major Sequoia National Park peaks reached by maintained trail, so go for it!

The route to the top of 11,204-foot Alta Peak is via a very steep trail. Efforts are rewarded by a panorama of peaks: Mt. Goddard and company to the north, the summits about Mineral King to the south, mighty Mt. Whitney to the east, and beyond the sometimes foggy, sometimes smoggy San Joaquin Valley, the Coast Range to the west.

Alta Meadow is the easier (though not easy) destination to reach. Situated on a ridge, the meadow, too, rewards the hiker with some good views.

This hike skips a few miles of Alta Trail. The reason? No good purpose is served by starting three miles farther away, and a thousand feet lower in elevation, and trudging a less-than-thrilling stretch of trail along Generals Highway.

DIRECTIONS: From Generals Highway, 3 miles north of Giant Village, take the Wolverton turnoff and proceed 1.5 miles to a large parking area and signed Lakes Trail.

THE HIKE: Climb concrete steps to an information board, trailhead and signed Lakes Trail. In just 0.1 mile, meet a path leading to the Lodgepole area. Keep on Lakes Trail and ascend a ridge amidst red fir forest. A mile out, the path ascends above Wolverton Creek and passes a lovely meadow. Curving southeast the path meets Panther Gap Trail 1.8 miles from the trailhead.

Join Panther Gap Trail and after another 1.1 mile reach Panther Gap (elevation 8,400 feet). Enjoy the good views (of Great Western Divide and the Kaweah River's Middle Fork) then continue east on Alta Trail, traveling from red fir forest into a brushier environs of manzanita and chinquapin.

Shortly after passing a junction with Seven-Mile Hill Trail (which leads south to the High Sierra Trail), reach Mehrten Meadow. The meadow, tucked in a bowl, has a small creek and some campsites. Another 1.3-mile ascent takes you over the 9,000-foot elevation mark and a trail junction. The left fork leads to Alta Peak, the right fork to Alta Meadow.

To Alta Peak: Ascend very steeply north on the trail. Thin air, and a nearly two thousand foot-climb in the next 2.6 miles mean very slow progress for even the well-conditioned hiker. Looming above is the granite dome of Tharps Rock. A 1,000-foot-elevation gain over rocky, pine-dotted slopes takes you to timberline. Near the summit, the trail fades to oblivion and you make your way over lichen-decorated slabs of granite to the very top. Savor the far-reaching panoramas as well as views of nearer terrain below to the north—Pear and Emerald lakes.

To Alta Meadow: The lower trail travels a mellow 1.7 mile (with only a modest elevation gain) to the large, enchanting ridgeline meadow.

From Alta Peak: a stunning panorama of pine-dotted slopes and rocky peaks.

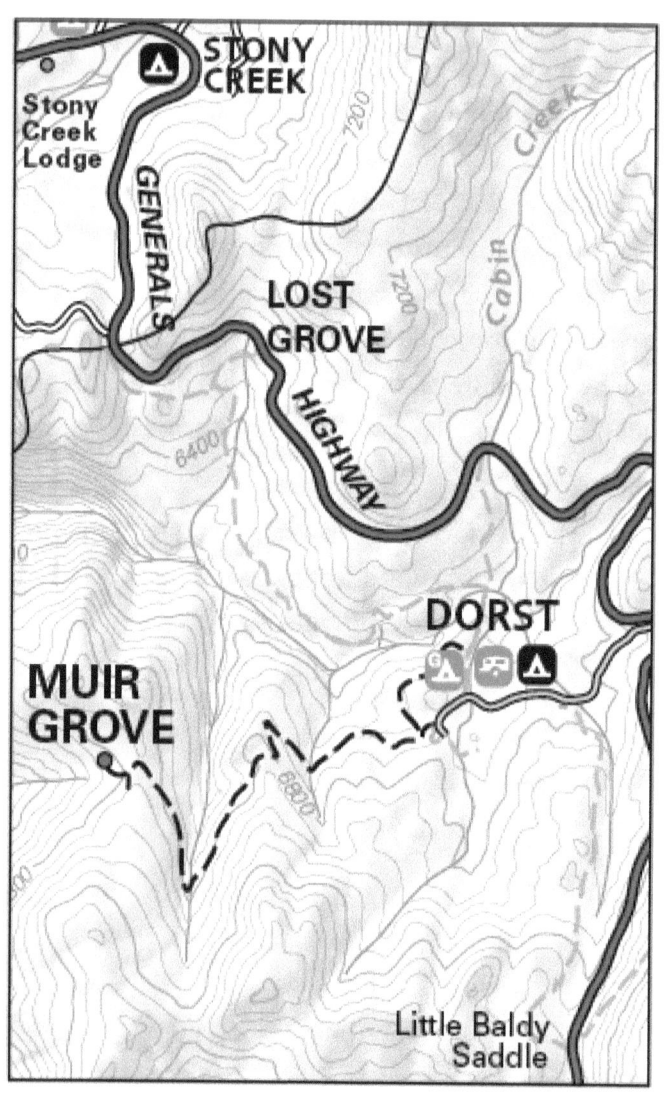

Muir Grove

Muir Grove Trail

4 miles round trip

These sequoias are off the beaten track. No roads come near. No tour buses, no parking lots, no crowds. Maybe this isolation makes Muir Grove so special.

It's not that isolated, though; the grove can be reached by an easy 2-mile walk from Dorst Creek Campground. Still, because it's a hike, not a highway, that visits the grove, few travelers take the time to walk to this magnificent stand of sequoias located in the northwest corner of the park.

John Muir's nature writing and conservation efforts helped to sway public and political opinions to create Sequoia and General Grant (the forerunner of Kings Canyon) national parks; it's a proper tribute to the great naturalist that Muir Grove was named for him.

The 215-acre grove is free of fencing, interpretive signs, named trees, pavement and parking lots. Expect quality not quantity. Marvel at a dozen or so sequoia accessible by trail; no footpath leads to the other trees in the grove. In early to mid-summer, the forest floor is often festooned with lupine, adding a complementary purple to the red-barked sequoia.

Muir Grove Trail offers a woodsy walk. The path leads through a Sierra forest of mixed conifers and along two mellow creeks. No sequoias are visible en route; it's pines that predominate.

Trailhead is Dorst Creek Campground, a large family-friendly favorite, complete with sites located beneath the trees and plenty of bear-proof food lockers. Yes, Dorst Creek is a favorite campground for hungry bears, too.

Dorst Creek Campground is also a trailhead (trail terminus, really) for 2.3-mile-long Lost Grove Trail that extends to a sequoia grove located near Generals Highway. It's a pretty enough pathway, amidst ferns and azaleas, cross creeks and meadows, but little used because the hike's chief attraction—Lost Grove—is only a short walk from the highway. Anything but "lost" or obscure, Lost Grove was the site of a Sequoia National Park entrance station before Kings Canyon National Park was established in 1940.

DIRECTIONS: From its junction with Highway 180 follow Generals Highway 17 miles to the turnoff for Dorst Creek Campground. Locate the signed beginning of Muir Grove Trail near the Group Camp area at a log bridge on the right side of the road.

THE HIKE: Begin a mild descent through a sugar pine, incense cedar and fir forest, soon following a tributary of Dorst Creek. The Dorst place names in these parts honor Captain Joseph Dorst, leader of the cavalry troop stationed here to protect Sequoia and General Grant national parks after they were created in 1890.

After meandering for 0.75 mile past ferns and wildflowers, the pleasant path then ascends a quarter-mile up a rocky ridge. You'll spot Muir Grove in the distance—on a nearby ridge. Descend into and climb out of a canyon before reaching the grove of huge sequoias.

The trail appears to continue, but actually disappears a short distance after the grove.

"Noblest of a noble race," is how the great naturalist John Muir described the mighty sequoia.

Spring is an ideal time to hike to the park's lovely, lower elevation attractions.

EVERY TRAIL TELLS A STORY.

II
Foothills

HIKE ON.

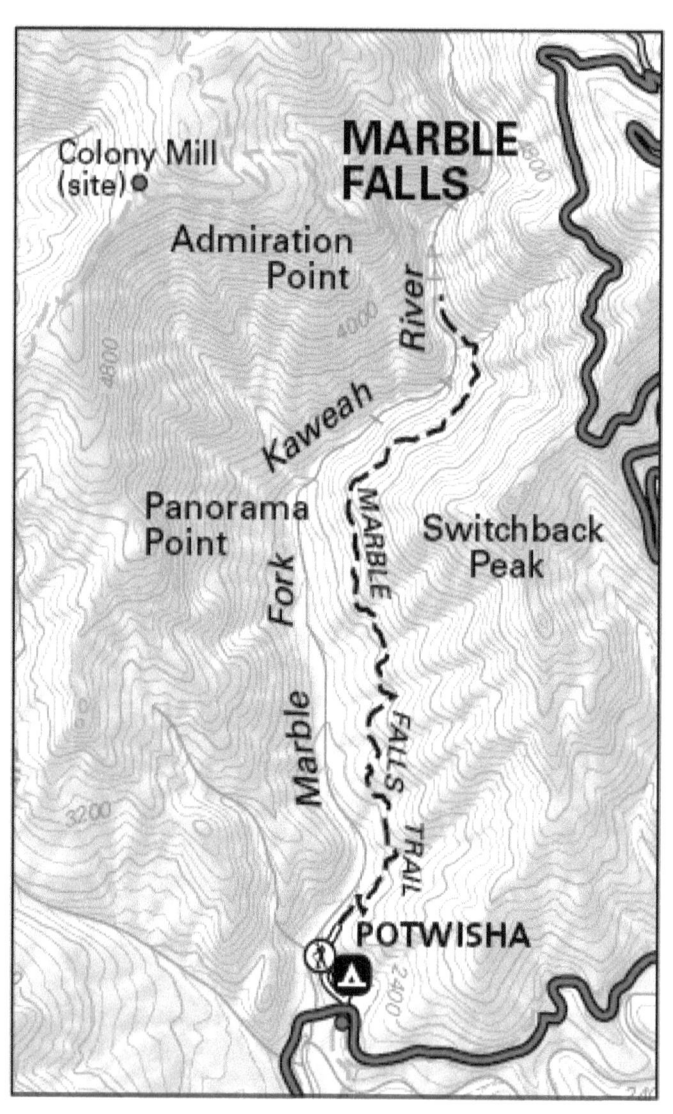

Marble Falls

Marble Fork Trail

From Potwisha Campground to Marble Falls is 7.8 miles round trip with 1,500-foot elevation gain

Depending on the year's snowfall and snowmelt, the Marble Fork of the Kaweah River can range from frisky and frothy to a downright raging torrent. From the trail that traces the canyon wall, hikers get great views of the pools and cascades bordered and channeled by the canyon's marble boulders.

Not only is the river an impressive sight, it produces an awesome sound—positively thunderous in spring. The trail to Marble Falls is a particularly splendid one to take in the springtime when the rest of park lies under a blanket of snow and the path is bordered by wildflowers.

The trail is open all year around but comes with a few warnings. First, it's hotter than Hades during the summer. And on my hikes here, I've spotted ticks, a rattlesnake and lots of poison oak—fauna and flora common in the foothills but rare in Sequoia and Kings Canyon national parks.

DIRECTIONS: From Sequoia National Park's Ash Mountain entrance, follow Highway 198/Generals Highway 3.8 miles northeast to the turnoff for Potwisha Campground. Park in spaces adjacent to a park maintenance facility located just across the highway from the campground.

THE HIKE: Cross Generals Highway and follow the Potwisha Campground loop to campsite 14. Follow a dirt road past warning signs about dogs and bears and past a barrier. Cross over a flume on a wooden bridge and parallel the aqueduct to the beginning of signed, single-track Marble Fork Trail.

Switchbacks ascend through oak woodland, shading some lovely ferns. A bit more than a mile out, the trail leaves the trees behind and rises into the chaparral.

After another 0.5 mile, the trail narrows and steepens. It can be nervous time for the hiker here because the trail is rocky and traces the canyon wall some 600 feet above the river.

The ascent mellows, even leveling out in a few stretches, but mostly it's a steady uphill pull. There's a bit of shade (oaks and the spring-blooming buckeye) en route, where the trail crosses a number of seasonal creeks.

Pause often to catch your breath and enjoy the great views down into the canyon. Hikers can hear the river, too, even though the trail is hundreds of feet above it.

After crossing one last creeklet, the path heads into the main canyon. As the trail nears the river, watch for outcroppings of white and gray marble that give this fork of the Kaweah its name. The trail ends at the river and below the falls.

Short paths lead to perches offering views of Marble Falls. It can be a dangerous undertaking to head upriver beyond the falls because the terrain is rough, the rock slick and the river fast-moving and powerful.

The Kaweah River thunders over polished white and gray marble. An awesome sight—and sound!

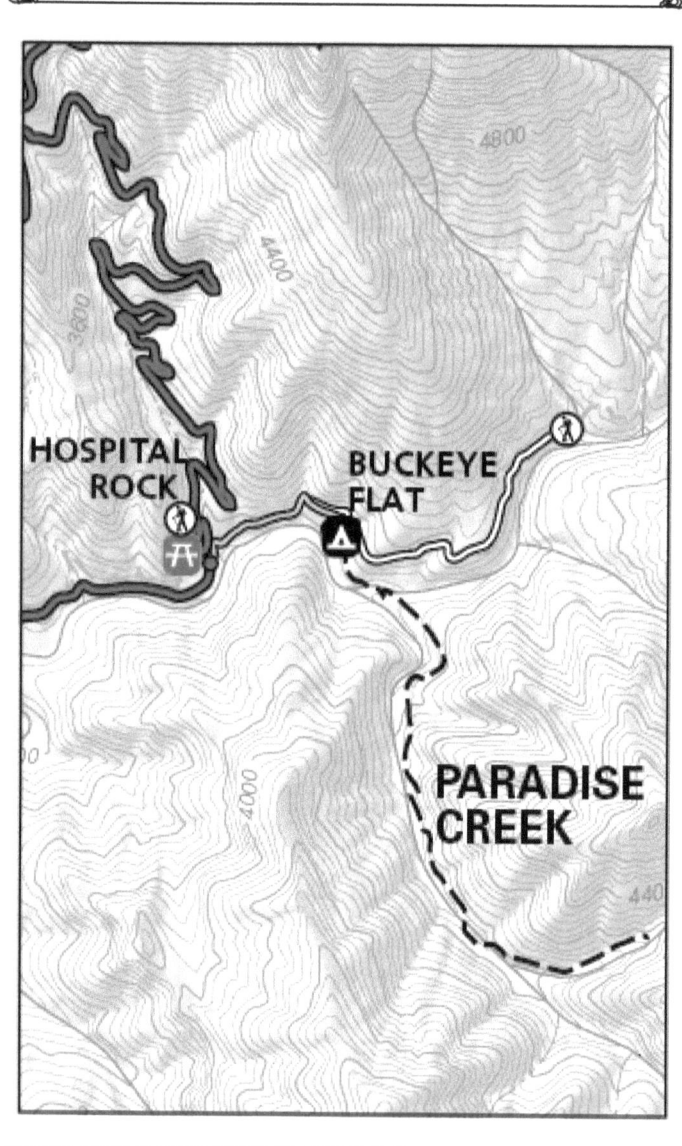

Paradise Creek

Paradise Creek Trail

From Buckeye Flat Campground to Paradise Creek is 3.6 miles round trip

Compared to other all-year foothill trails leading across open, sun-baked slopes, Paradise Creek is a much shadier route through a mixed forest of oak, ponderosa pines and even some spring-blooming buckeyes. Wildflowers and small waterfalls and pools along the creek are added attractions.

Swimming is the big draw of Paradise Creek. The Kaweah River can be gnarly but the gentler Paradise Creek offers quiet pools for wading and cooling off.

When Paradise Creek Trail was constructed in the 1920s, it extended all the way from the Middle Fork of the Kaweah River to Mineral King. However, once the road to Mineral King was built it found little favor with hikers and its upper length was abandoned in the 1960s and these days is maintained for only 2.5 miles or so.

The trail begins at Hospital Rock, named in 1873 when James Everton stayed here to recover from a shotgun blast meant for a bear. Check out the bedrock mortars and rock art left behind by the native people, who lived here in a village (population of 500 or so).

DIRECTIONS: From Sequoia National Park's Ash Mountain entrance, follow Highway 198/Generals Highway 6.2 miles northeast to Hospital Rock on the left side of the highway and the turnoff on the right for Buckeye Flat Campground. Park in the Hospital Rock (Day-use parking is prohibited in the campground, which is closed, along with the entry road from late fall until early summer.)

THE HIKE: Walk 0.6 mile along the narrow paved road to the campground. You'll get good views of the river and of Moro Rock, which has an odd and narrow profile from this angle. Look for the trailhead at the south end of the campground opposite site #28.

From the campground, the path makes a modest ascent and descent amidst oak and ponderosa pine to reach a handsome footbridge over the Middle Fork of the Kaweah River. Gaze up at Paradise Ridge to the south, towering nearly 5,000 feet above the river. On the other side of the 40-foot long bridge, note a short path leading down-river to a huge swimming hole.

Signed Paradise Creek Trail offers a glimpse of the creek and large pools and begins ascending via a couple of switchbacks. Get excellent vistas of the Middle Fork of the Kaweah. The trail soon mellows out and parallels the creek. Plenty of natural swimming pools en route, if you're so inclined.

About a mile from the trailhead, reach the first crossing of Paradise Creek. (In times of high water, this can be a challenge to ford so use caution.) The path heads along the west bank then re-crosses the creek in 0.2 mile. After this the trail is not maintained, though the determined hiker can continue along faint and brush-overgrown trail.

Check out the mortar holes and rock art near Hospital Rock and learn more about the native people who lived there.

Contemplate Mineral King's beauty.

EVERY TRAIL TELLS A STORY.

III
Mineral King

HIKE ON.

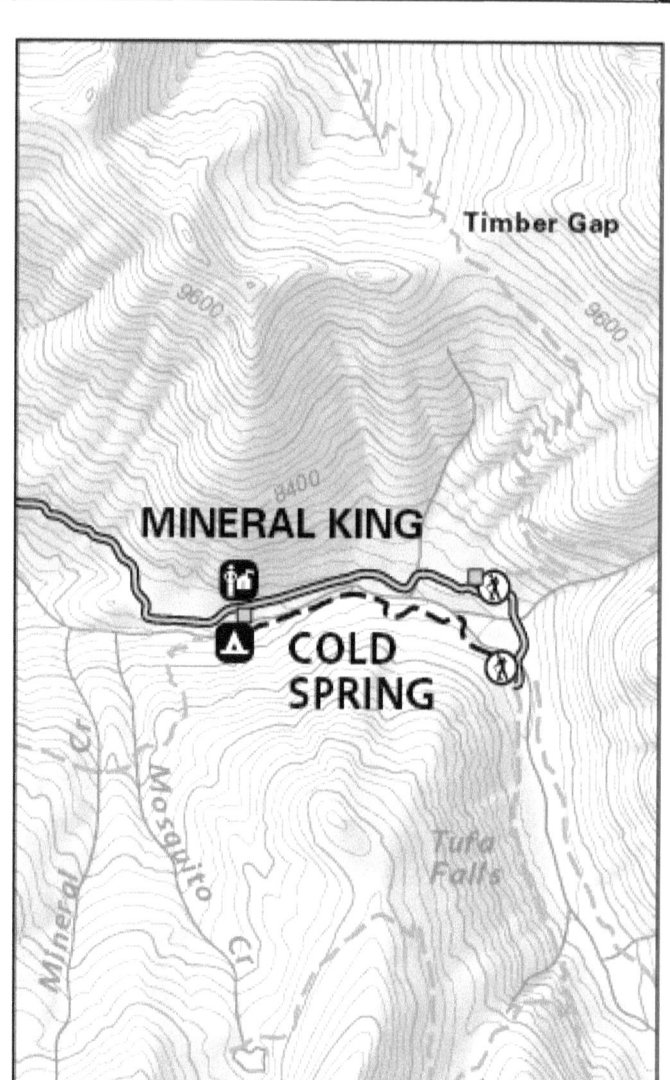

Mineral King Valley

Cold Springs Trail

2 miles round trip

Mellow and magical, Cold Springs Trail (formerly a nature trail with interpretive signs) offers an easy introduction to the beauties of Mineral King Valley, including a tour of the valley's characteristic trees—red fir, juniper, aspen and cottonwood—and exploration of a meadow and the riparian flora along the river. Traipse the wildflower-lined trail along the banks of the East Fork of the Kaweah River and enjoy dramatic vistas (particularly at sunset!) of the Sawtooth Range.

DIRECTIONS: Park in the lot opposite the entrance to Cold Springs Campground. The trail begins at Campsite 6.

THE HIKE: Hike across meadows and through aspen groves along the Kaweah River into Mineral King Valley via switchbacks, wooden walkways and rock steps. Trail's end is the parking area near the Eagle Lake trailhead.

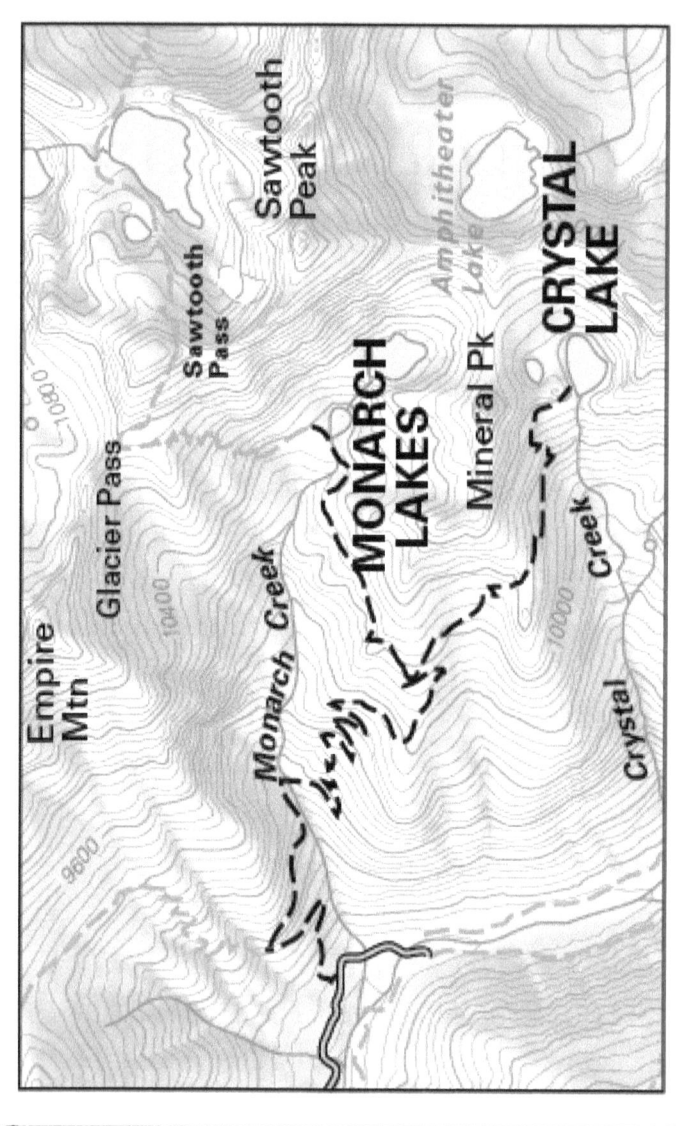

Monarch Lakes & Crystal Lakes

Monarch Lakes, Crystal Lakes Trails

To Monarch Lakes is 8.4 miles round trip with 2,600-foot elevation gain; to Crystal Lake is 9.8 miles round trip with 3,000-foot elevation gain

For a great intro to Mineral King, a gorgeous, avalanche-scoured valley ringed by rugged 11,000-foot peaks, hit the trail to Monarch Lakes and Crystal Lakes.

From the Sawtooth Trailhead, lung-popping ascents through thin air are required to reach the two superb sets of high-country lakes. The hike to both lakes shares a common trailhead and first 3.5 miles of trail.

DIRECTIONS: From Highway 198, follow Mineral King Road 23 miles to Mineral King Ranger Station, then one more mile to the Sawtooth Trailhead Parking area.

THE HIKE: The no-nonsense trail begins its steady ascent. A few hundred yards up the trail look for a small waterfall on Monarch Creek. A side trail leads southeast to the base of the fall.

A half-mile out, pass a junction with Timber Gap Trail and, after a mile, reach Groundhog Meadow. Marmots inhabit the meadow, seasonally brightened by Indian paintbrush, corn lily, and shooting star.

Cross Monarch Creek and begin a steep ascent over slopes spiked with red fir and juniper. As you ascend switchbacks into the forest, enjoy those vistas of Mineral King Valley. The switchbacks end but the vigorous climb continues to the ridgeline dividing the Monarch Creek drainage from Chihuahua Bowl. The grade lessens for a time then switchbacks up to Monarch Lakes/Crystal Lake Junction 3.5 miles from the trailhead.

TO MONARCH LAKES: The ascent mellows as you probe Monarch Canyon, where snow often lingers into summer. Look up ahead to towering, toothsome Sawtooth Peak (12,343 feet) and the notch on its shoulder—Sawtooth Pass. Negotiate shifting shale, cross Monarch Creek and arrive at the smaller of the two Monarch lakes. Looming over "Little" Monarch Lake is 11,615-foot Mineral Peak. Some rock-scrambling leads to the larger Monarch lake.

TO CRYSTAL LAKE: Ascend the rugged path a severe 0.25 mile to rocky Chihuahua Bowl, an avalanche-scoured basin. Here you'll find piled tailings, stone foundations and the sealed entrance to Chihuahua Mine. The mine, a difficult-to-work operation (with no water supply) failed to produce the volume of silver and gold its investors had hoped.

More climbing brings leads to the foxtail pine–dotted ridgetop, about 0.75 mile from the trail junction. Note diminutive Cobalt Lake below; an unsigned trail leads to it.

Crystal Lake Trail contours along rocky slopes for a short distance, and then climbs again via tight switchbacks to a junction with the short side trail that leads to Upper Crystal Lake. Continue straight for Lower Crystal Lake. Lower Crystal Lake, nestled in a rocky bowl below some awesome peaks, is yet another Sierra Lake made more reservoir-like by the Mt. Whitney Power Company. From the lake's dam, built in 1903, enjoy excellent Mineral King vistas.

Marmots rule the rocks all around Mineral King.

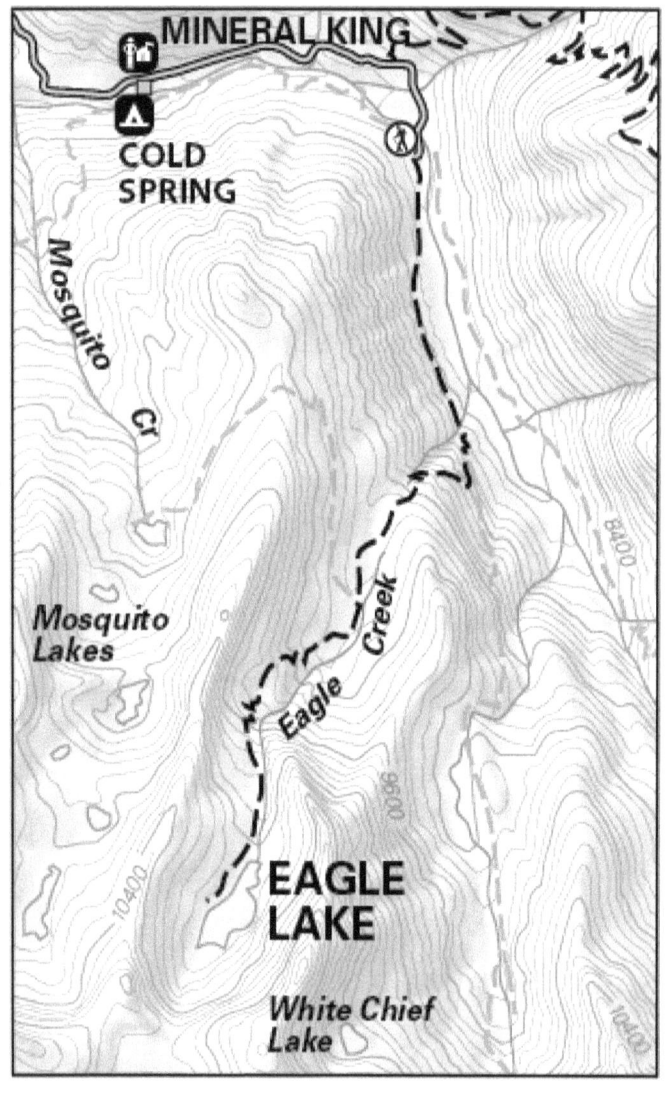

Eagle Lake

Eagle Lake Trail

7.2 miles round trip with 2,200-foot elevation gain

Eagle Lake, a popular weekend backpacker destination, is reached by one of Mineral King's easier trails. Relatively easier, that is. A 2,200-foot gain at high altitude in 3.5 miles is a good workout to say the least.

The lake lies in cirque, a basin formed by glacial erosion. When the light is right, the lake mirrors some of its scenic surroundings: weathered foxtail pines and polished granite walls, their shaded cracks and crevices patched by long-lingering snow.

Eagle, like many a Sierra lake, was "improved" to render it more reservoir-like. The Mt. Whitney Power Company built a rock dam to better control waters flowing down to its hydroelectric plant located near Three Rivers.

The moderately steep path has three branches: to Eagle Lake; to Mosquito Lakes (see hike description); to White Chief Canyon.

En route to Eagle Lake, you'll encounter two strange waterways. The path crosses Spring Creek, which emerges as if from nowhere. Geologists speculate that it's of subterranean origin. If the sudden appearance of Spring Creek isn't strange enough, Eagle Lake Trail hikers also witness the disappearance of Eagle Creek into a large sinkhole. The creek reappears down the hillside, leading to speculation that is channeled through a network of underground passageways in the marble rock below ground and emerges as…Spring Creek?

Very mysterious.

Experienced hikers, familiar with cross-country travel, can make a loop of this hike: climb a ridge from Eagle Lake then descend into Mosquito Lakes Basin. You'll arrive at Mosquito Lake #4 and follow the lake chain north until you join the Mosquito Lakes Trail that returns you to Mineral King.

DIRECTIONS: From Highway 198, about 3 miles northeast of the town of Three Rivers, turn right (east) on Mineral King Road. (If you drive up to the park's Ash Mountain entrance station, you've gone a tad too far; double back.) The mostly paved road (it reverts to dirt in several places en route) leads about 24 miles to the Mineral King Ranger Station.

Continue east on Mineral King Road another 1.3 miles and across a wooden bridge to the trailhead parking area.

THE HIKE: Join the signed trail and soon view the restored "Honeymoon Cabin," circa 1914. The path leads south along the East Fork of the Kaweah River and in 0.3 mile crosses the strange Spring Creek on a wooden footbridge. Look for Tufa Falls, a cascade so named for high levels of calcium carbonate in the waters.

One mile out, at a junction with the trail to Eagle Lake/Mosquito Lakes, turn right, tackling steep switchbacks that climb a half-mile over fir-clad mountainside. Observe Eagle Creek's disappearing act into a sinkhole and continue across a meadow to the junction with Mosquito Lakes Trail, two miles out. (See Mosquito Lakes hike.)

Continue southwest toward Eagle Lake. Staying west of Eagle Creek, the trail switchbacks steeply, climbing white granite slopes and finally reaching the outlet of Eagle Lake.

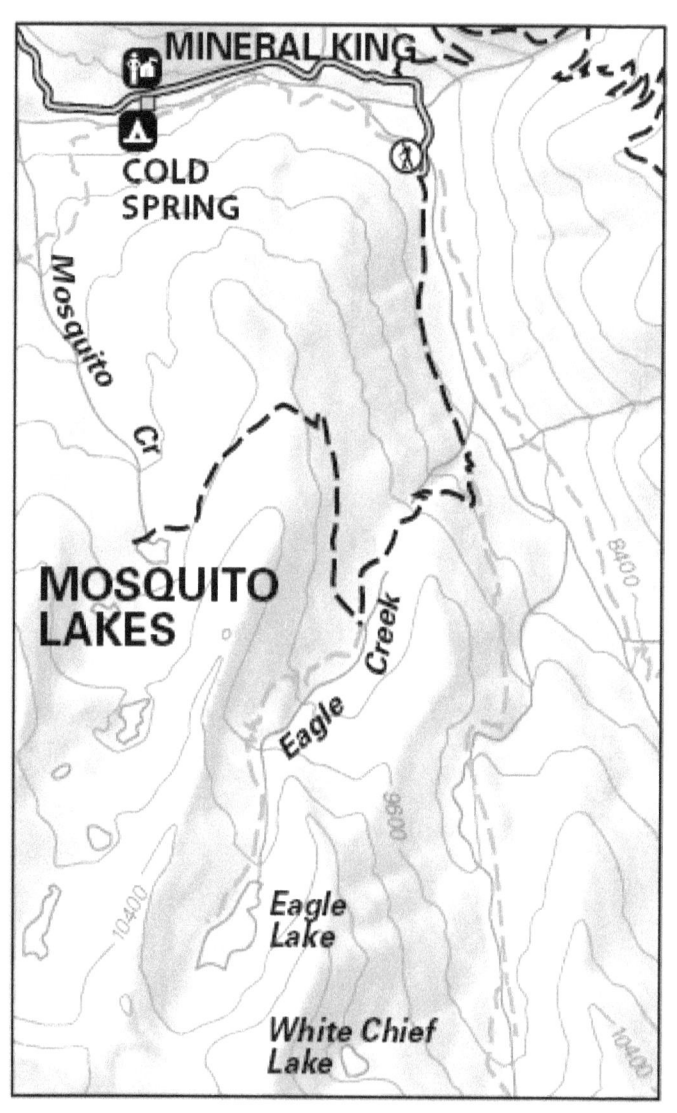

Mosquito Lakes

Eagle Lake, Mosquito Lakes Trails

To first Mosquito Lake is 7.2 miles round trip; to fifth Mosquito Lake is 10.2 miles round trip

Tucked in a little valley at the base of Hengst Peak, five Mosquito Lakes beckon the day hiker and backpacker. Each glacier-carved lake fills a rocky bowl and seems to have its own special quality.

This hike begins with the path to Eagle Lake which has three branches: Eagle Lake (see hike description), Mosquito Lakes and White Chief Canyon.

Mosquito Lakes Trail ascends in stairstep fashion from one lake to another. Actually, only the first lake (where no camping is allowed) is reached by maintained trail. Beyond Mosquito Lake #1, follow sketchy paths, cairns and blazes to reach the upper lakes.

In the warmer months, expect hordes of the mosquitoes that gave the lakes their name. Take precautions and plenty of bug repellant to fully enjoy this hike.

DIRECTIONS: From Highway 198, about three miles northeast of the town of Three Rivers, turn right (east) on Mineral King Road. (If you drive up to the park's Ash Mountain entrance station, you've gone a tad too far; double back.) The mostly paved road (it reverts to dirt in several places en route) leads about 24 miles to the Mineral King Ranger Station. Continue east on Mineral King Road another 1.3 miles farther and across a wooden bridge to the trailhead parking area. Warning: Local marmots have developed a taste for rubber and sometimes gnaw on vehicle belts and hoses.

THE HIKE: Join the signed trail and soon view the restored "Honeymoon Cabin," circa 1914. The path leads south along the East Fork of the Kaweah River and in 0.3 mile crosses the strange Spring Creek on a wooden footbridge. Look for Tufa Falls, a cascade so named for high levels of calcium carbonate in the waters.

One mile out, at a junction with the trail to Eagle Lake/Mosquito Lakes, turn right, tackling steep switchbacks that climb a half-mile over fir-clad mountainside. Observe Eagle Creek's disappearing act into a sinkhole and continue across a meadow to the junction with Mosquito Lakes Trail, 2 miles out.

At the junction, Mosquito Lake-bound hikers stay right, traversing a lodgepole pine-fringed meadow. Soon, begin some serious climbing, tackling a ridge with steep switchbacks and getting good views of Sawtooth Peak. You make your way to a saddle, nearly 3 miles out.

Now the path switchbacks down through dense red fir forest before reaching the boulder-strewn shore of Lower Mosquito Lake.

Head right along the lakeshore, cross Mosquito Creek, and follow the use trail up a narrow forested valley, then over a rocky section to the second Mosquito Lake. Cross the lake's outlet creek and begin following ducks up the forested mountainside to the next "stairstep."

Continue up-valley, hiking east of Mosquito #3 and west of Mosquito #4, considered to have the best campsites. Mosquito #5, largest of the lot, has the most dramatic scenery.

Rub on plenty of repellant and take a hike to Mosquito Lakes—a far more attractive destination than its name suggest.

Boole Tree appears all the more awesome because of its isolated location.

EVERY TRAIL TELLS A STORY.

IV
Giant Sequoia National Monument

HIKE ON.

TheTrailmaster.com

Giant Sequoia National Monument

Boole Tree Trail

2 miles out and back or 2.5 mile-loop with 500-foot elevation gain.

Once upon a time, Converse Basin nurtured one of the most majestic, and quite possibly the largest, groves of giant sequoias in creation.

Then the axe fell. Hard. Even by the cut-and-run logging standards of the time (1880s), the clear-cut of Converse Basin was a merciless assault on the earth's largest living things. This wanton destruction of the giant sequoias was not even that profitable; by some accounts, fewer than half the trees destroyed ever reached mills to be sawn into lumber.

What's left today is Stump Meadow, a lovely, but somewhat surreal landscape populated with huge, ghostly stumps and a bare handful of still-standing Sequoias. In what may be the height of irony, the tallest survivor, 269-foot high Boole Tree, bears the name of the general manager of the Sanger Lumber Company, Frank Boole, believed to have ordered this particular tree spared.

Once thought to be the world's tallest sequoia, Boole Tree is now ranked as the 8th tallest. Estimated to be more than 2,000 years old, the behemoth is the largest tree in any of America's national forests. Boole Tree's ground perimeter of 113 feet (!) is the greatest girth of all sequoias.

Boole Tree's awesome stature is accentuated by its isolated location above the Kings River and by the way it towers over the rest of the forest. An enjoyable family-friendly loop trail leads to Boole Tree and delivers wonderful views of Kings Canyon and the park's high peaks.

Add to your visit with two more stops in Converse Basin. On the drive to the Boole Tree trailhead, stop for a look at Muir Snag, oldest-known giant sequoia. The long-dead tree, estimated to have been more than 3,000 years old when it perished, was discovered by and named for John Muir.

General Noble Tree stood 285 feet high and measured 26 feet in diameter when it was cut down in 1893 and sent to the Columbian Exposition in Chicago. A short walk on flat trail brings you to the 20-foot high Chicago Stump. (Look for the signed turnoff off Highway 180 about 4.5 miles north of Grant Grove Village.)

DIRECTIONS: The signed turnoff for the Boole Tree is located off Highway 180 about 6 miles north of Grant Village. Turn left on Converse Road (also known as Forest Road 13S55) and continue 2.5 miles to road's end and plenty of parking.

THE HIKE: Begin your ascent on the well-built path across hillsides cloaked in bracken fern and manzanita. Switchbacks and railroad tie stairsteps aid the climb, which passes through a mixed forest of white fir, oaks, incense cedar and a few young sequoias.

Just short of a mile out, crest a ridge and catch a glimpse of the Middle Fork of the Kings River. Descend to a junction with a short connector trail leading down to the base of Boole Tree.

Return the same way or add a half-mile of hiking by making this a loop trip and getting excellent views of Kings River Canyon.

*General Grant:
"The Nation's Christmas Tree"*

EVERY TRAIL TELLS A STORY.

V
KINGS CANYON NATIONAL PARK

HIKE ON.

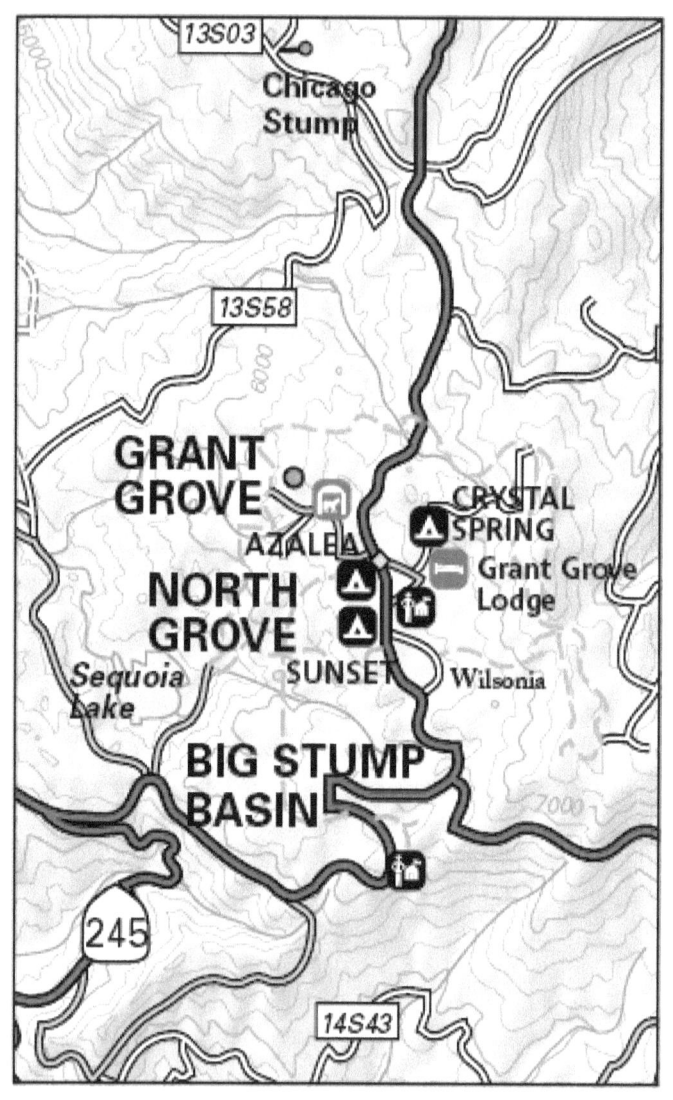

Grant Grove

General Grant Tree Trail

1 mile round trip

General Grant Tree, the world's third-largest tree, was the showpiece of General Grant National Park, forerunner of Kings Canyon, set aside in 1890. In the General's neighborhood are many other notable sequoias, which can be explored by an interpretive loop trail.

Designated "the Nation's Christmas Tree" in 1926, the General Grant Tree is still the site where Christmas services are held beneath its boughs. Congress proclaimed the tree a National Shrine in 1956, a living memorial to the nation's war dead.

DIRECTIONS: From Highway 180 at the Kings Canyon National Park Big Stump entrance, take the Azalea Campground/Grant Tree turnoff and proceed a mile to the large parking lot. (If camping at adjacent Azalea Campground you can avoid the heavily-trafficked Grant Tree parking lot by taking a connector trail to the trailhead.)

THE HIKE: Purchase a pamphlet at the trailhead if you wish and begin the 16-stop interpretive trail. Take the right fork of the paved path and soon arrive at Robert E. Lee Tree, ranked #13 on the Largest Sequoias List. (Many sequoias were named for Civil War and post Civil War-era personages because the region was explored and preservation efforts began during that period.)

Continue past young sequoias (planted in 1949) that range from 10 to nearly 90 feet in height; this height variation is an obvious example of the role of sunlight in stimulating the growth of individual trees. Also behold the sequoia's forest companions: sugar pine, ponderosa pine, incense cedar and white fir.

Trail namesake General Grant Tree is just plain big: 267.4 feet high, and an estimated 2,000 years old. While third in size, it's Number One in base diameter—more than 40 feet!

Continue on a dirt pathway that loops around the tree and perhaps take a side trail to the Vermont Log, a 246-footer that had a Leaning Tower of Pisa lean before giving in to gravity in 1985.

Proceed to Gamlin Cabin, built by pioneer logging brothers Thomas and Israel Gamlin in the late 1860s. The cabin later served as the first ranger station in General Grant National Park.

Centennial Stump is what remains of a 1,800-year-old giant sequoia felled for display at

America's 1876 Centennial Exhibition in Philadelphia. A 16-foot section was sliced off, split into sections, and reassembled at the exhibition; attendees refused to believe that a tree could grow that large and branded it the "California Hoax."

Fallen Monarch, a horizontal giant, was used as a hotel, saloon, and later as a stable for the horses of the U.S. Cavalry, who patrolled the national park in its earliest days.

Pass Lincoln Tree and, as you approach the trailhead, look toward the west side of the lot, for the Twin Sisters, two trees fused together and on the east side for a grouping known as the Happy Family. Naturalists figure these specimens grew up together after a fire cleared out the area and gave them room to grow and grow and grow.

Grant Grove visitors, circa 1900.

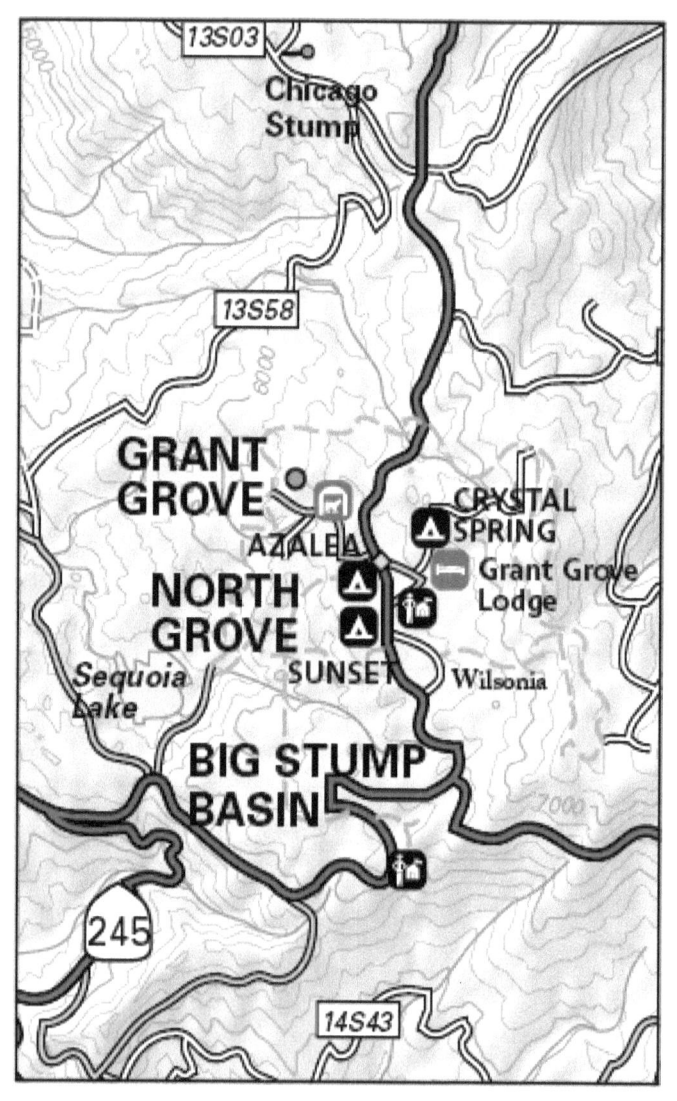

North Grove

North Grove Loop Trail

North Grove Loop Trail is 2.5 miles round trip with 300-foot elevation gain

Not far from the maddening crowd—in fact, just across the vast parking lot for Grant Grove—tranquility, in the form of North Grove, awaits. Wander through a peaceful forest of sugar pine, white fir and scattered sequoia, the latter seeming all the more grand in the company with trees of lesser girth and stature.

This is a great add-on to the General Grant Tree walk for those who want a little more hiking.

DIRECTIONS: From Highway 180 at the Kings Canyon National Park Big Stump entrance, take the Azalea Campground/Grant Tree turnoff and proceed a mile to the large parking lot. North Grove Trail begins at the far side of the recreational vehicle/bus parking area.

(If you happen to be camping at adjacent Azalea Campground you can avoid the heavily-trafficked Grant Tree parking lot by taking a connector trail to the trailhead.)

THE HIKE: Start with a brief 0.1-mile descent on a paved road before veering right on signed North Grove Loop Trail. Your path, an old dirt road, descends 0.75 mile through a mixed forest of incense cedar, sugar pine and sequoia to the bottom of a hill and a junction with Old Millwood Road.

(This now-retiring road once extended to Millwood, an 1890s mill town from which sequoia logs were sent by flume down to the San Joaquin Valley town of Sanger, near Fresno. It's far from my favorite hike, but those with an interest in history might like to trek the one lane dirt road, which descends steeply 2.3 miles to the site of the old logging town.)

Past its junction with Millwood Road, North Grove Trail ascends south and east to a more distinct junction. Turn right and follow the road 0.25 mile around lovely Lion Meadow to intersect Dead Giant Trail, located about 1.25 miles from the trailhead.

Take the right (northwest), lower leg of the path that leads 0.2 mile to the Dead Giant, a towering, hollow, but still-standing sequoia.

The trail curves south then west to a signed side trail leading to a vista point overlooking Sequoia

Lake. Now appearing as a brilliant blue gem, surrounded by pines, the lake was actually created as a reservoir in 1889 when the Sanger Lumber Company dammed Sequoia Creek. The lake stored and released water to fill the company's flume, which floated logs more than 50 miles down to the Central Valley town of Sanger.

Backtrack to the main trail and descend east through the forest back to the closed road. Bear left (north), following the road past junctions with both legs of North Grove Trail back to the trailhead.

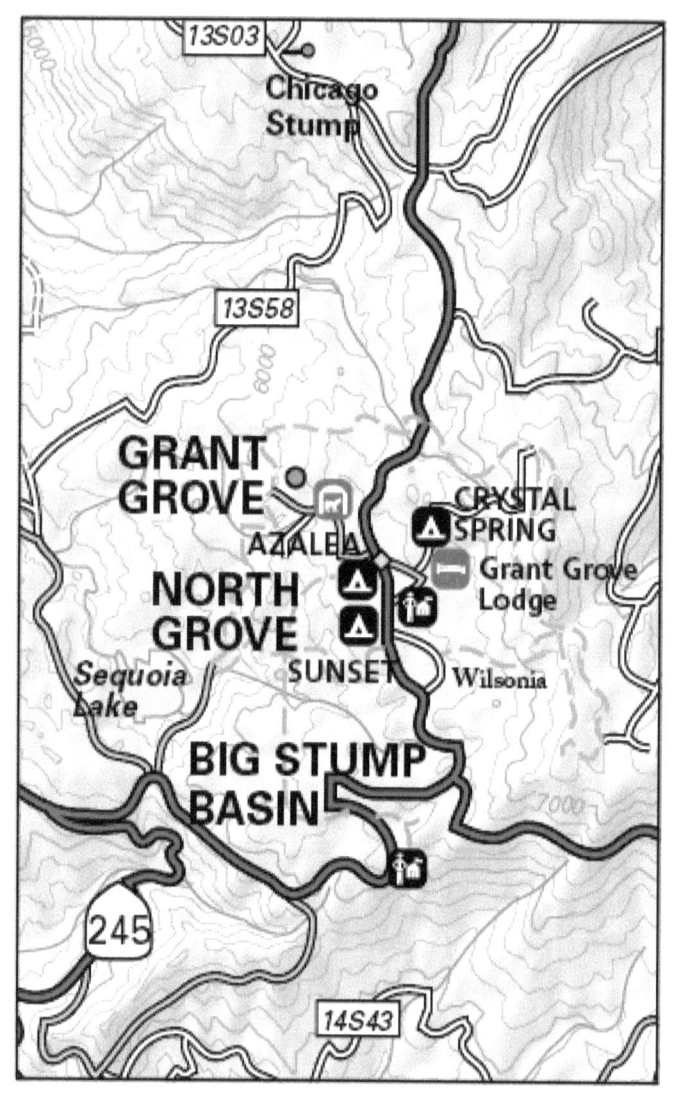

Big Stump Basin

Big Stump Trail

1 mile round trip with 200-foot elevation gain

Big Stump Trail is an intriguing nature trail, complete with a great history lesson, regenerating forest and a reminder that folks had a different environmental ethic in the 1880s.

Highlights are blackened but still-standing Burnt Monarch, Mark Twain Stump (no joke: the tree was 26-feet wide and 1,700 years old when felled in 1881) and Shattered Giant, now a trail bridge.

DIRECTIONS: From Big Stump Entrance Station, drive north for 0.6 mile north on Highway 180 to the Big Stump parking area. The unsigned trail begins at some steps by the restroom.

THE HIKE: The path angles south and east (with a detour to the Smith-Comstock Mill Site) to Big Stump Entrance Station. A return leg leads across the highway and visits Sawed Tree.

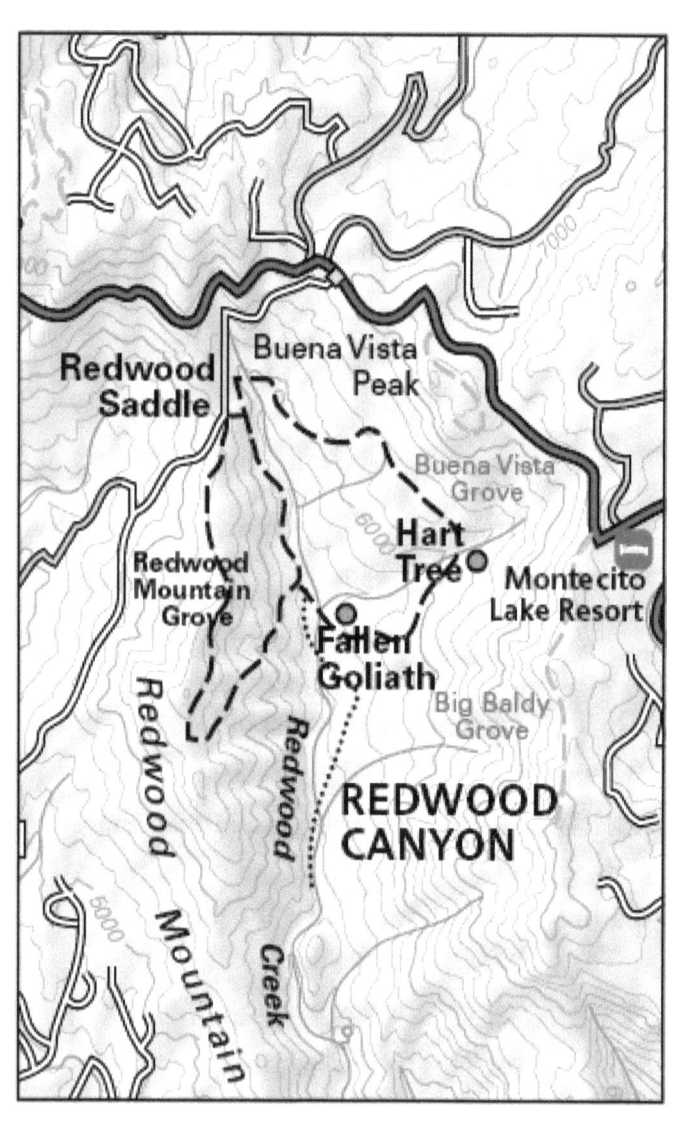

Redwood Canyon

Redwood Canyon, Hart Tree Trails

6.5 mile loop with 700-foot elevation gain; return via Sugar Bowl is 9-mile loop with 1,200-foot gain

The largest sequoia groves on the planet are found in Redwood Canyon in Kings Canyon National Park. More than 15,000 big trees spread over 4,000 acres and hiking is the only way to visit them.

Sixteen miles of trail weave among the extensive old-growth groves and meander along Redwood Creek. The trails offer hikers a kind of wilderness experience not possible from the awesome, but extremely popular groves in Sequoia National Park.

From a hiker's perspective, the sequoias en route sure seem more densely congregated than elsewhere in the park. The sequoia's creek-side companions are quite colorful: in spring, dogwood blooms along with purple lupine, and in autumn the forest lights up with the red and gold leaves of the aspen.

Sequoias aren't the only big trees in Redwood Canyon. Sugar pines can be as tall or taller than neighboring sequoia and have much larger cones—measuring 10 to 24 inches long—longest of all trees.

If you're short of time, hike out and back through Redwood Canyon—a 4-mile round trip jaunt on a trail paralleling Redwood Creek. Otherwise choose among stellar loop trips with plenty of sights to see: Tunnel Tree (the trail goes through it), Hart Tree (a top 20 sequoia), and a hollowed-out sequoia once used as a cabin.

My favorite loop visits Hart Tree and Fallen Goliath and returns via Redwood Canyon. Consider a longer return through the Sugar Bowl, characterized as "a grove within a grove," for its dense stands of young sequoia.

DIRECTIONS: From the Big Stump entry to Kings Canyon National Park, continue on Highway 180 1.5 miles to Generals Highway. Turn right and drive 3 miles to Quail Flat and a junction with the paved road to Hume Lake on the left. Turn right on dirt Redwood Saddle Road, descending amidst great sequoias 1.7 miles to a junction; fork left to the parking lot and signed trailhead.

THE HIKE: Walk down the wide forest path 0.3 mile to a signed junction. Bear left, crossing and re-crossing tributaries of fern-lined Redwood Creek.

About a mile out, reach Barton's Post Camp, site of a logging operation in the late 1800s.

Hike another mile to lush and lovely Hart Meadow, and then to and through Tunnel Tree (a hollowed-out sequoia log) to meet the short (100-yard) spur trail to Hart Tree at the 3.2-mile mark. After visiting the tree, largest in the grove, return to the main trail and descend to Fallen Goliath, a truly ancient tree now serving as a "nursery log" for young sequoias.

The path descends to Redwood Creek and a junction with Redwood Canyon Trail. Head right, up-creek and soon (0.1 mile) reach a junction with Sugar Bowl Trail; go left to extend your outing with a hike up and around Redwood Mountain. Otherwise continue up-canyon parallel to the creek. When you return to the junction with Hart Tree Trail, bear left and retrace your steps to the trailhead.

Hart Tree, 278 feet tall, ranks as the world's 26th largest tree.

Meander the gentle side of the park to lovely Zumwalt Meadow.

EVERY TRAIL TELLS A STORY.

VI
CEDAR GROVE

HIKE ON.

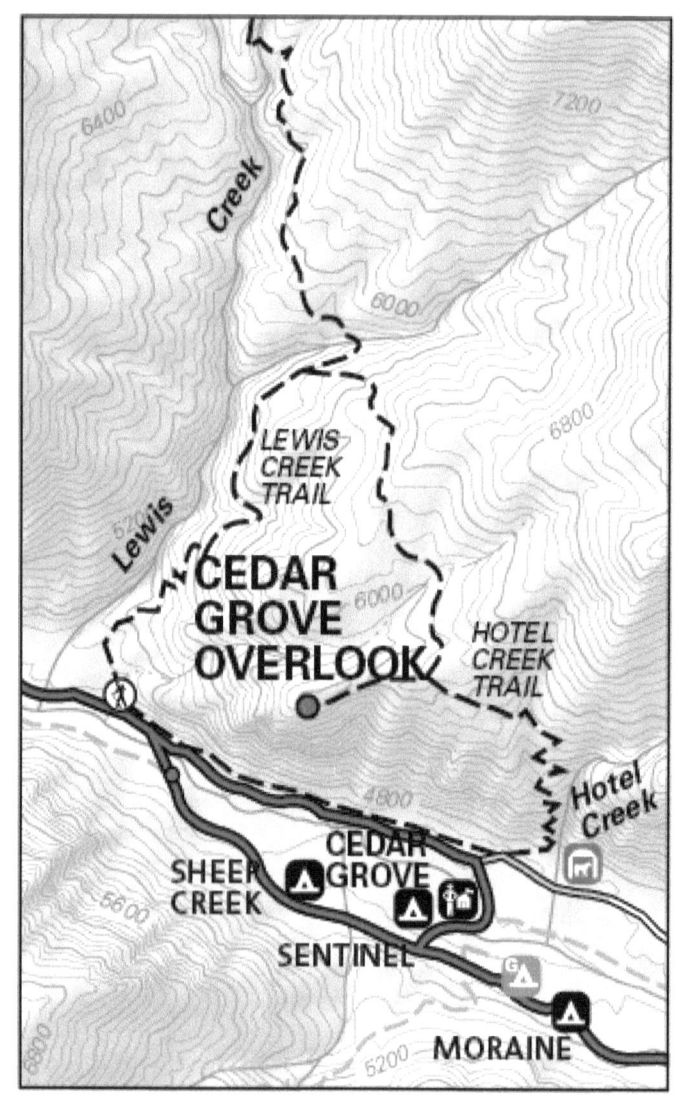

CEDAR GROVE OVERLOOK

HOTEL CREEK, LEWIS CREEK TRAILS

From Cedar Grove Village to Overlook is 3.8 miles round trip with 1,200-foot elevation gain; return via Lewis Creek Trail is 7.7 miles round trip

Enjoy great vistas of the length and depth of Kings Canyon as well as the dramatic peaks of the Monarch Wilderness from Cedar Grove Overlook. Some hikers refer to the vista point as Kings Canyon Overlook—for obvious reasons. The views are pretty terrific en route, so the leg-weary can take in the sights, cut the hike short before reaching the Overlook.

Extend the hike with a return via Lewis Creek Trail, a path that gets lots of equestrian use along its lower lengths. Whether you hike the shorter out-and-back to the Overlook or a longer loop, get an early start because after the first 0.5 mile or so of woodsy walking, this is a mostly shadeless hike.

DIRECTIONS: Follow Highway 180 to Cedar Grove Village. Follow the signs for the visitor center and Cedar Grove Lodge, continue 0.25 mile on the main road past the lodge, turn right, and soon look left for the parking lot for the Hotel Creek/Lewis Creek trailhead.

THE HIKE: Lewis Creek Trail (optional return route) leads left while Hotel Creek Trail leads right through mixed woodland of oak and pine. Just into the first (of many!) switchbacks, look for a side trail dropping to pools and cascades of Hotel Creek.

All too soon, the trail leaves behind the trees and travels sunny exposed slopes.

Zigzag along dozens of steep switchbacks gaining vistas of Kings Canyon, deepest canyon in the continental U.S., as well as dramatic Sentinel Ridge capped by Sentinel Dome.

At the signed junction, about 1.5 steep miles from the trailhead, bear left on Overlook Trail and hike 0.4 mile to the overlook. Unpack your lunch and enjoy the view down to Cedar Grove and the panorama of peaks.

Retrace your steps to the trailhead or opt to hike north from the Overlook/Hotel Creek Trail junction. Heading north, it's good news for the hiker as the trail leads through a yellow pine forest. Shade or at least partial shade! The pines frame views of the Monarch Divide and Monarch Wilderness summits.

It's mellow, fairly flat walking on Hotel Creek Trail, the path making only one brief ascent before intersecting Lewis Creek Trail amidst ponderosa pine and cedar.

(Strong and experienced hikers could consider hiking north—another shady 1.6 miles to Comb Creek for a dip in is shallow pools or hike one more mile for even better swimming and picnicking at Lewis Creek.)

Southbound Lewis Creek Trail descends via long switchbacks and parallels Lewis Creek. Much ceanothus blankets the slopes where chaparral plants have replaced the yellow pine forest that burned in a 1980 blaze.

At the Lewis Creek Trailhead by Highway 180, you must walk a final 1.8 miles eastbound on Lewis Creek Trail or along the road to Cedar Grove to close the loop. Not the most interesting way to end a good hike, for sure.

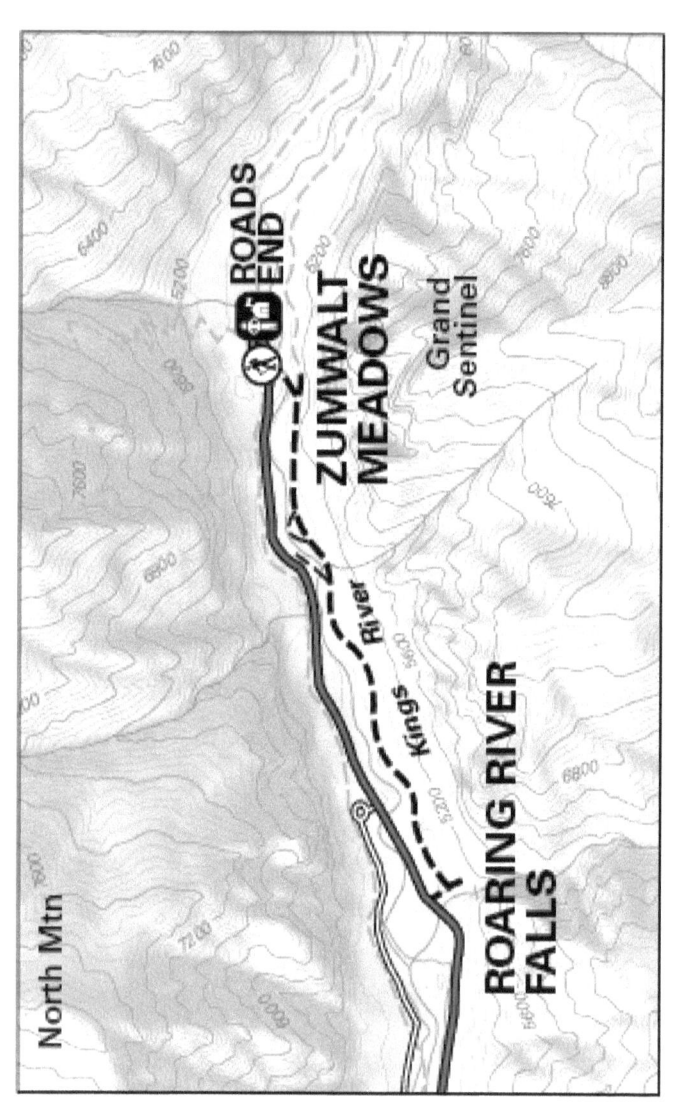

Zumwalt Meadow & Roaring River Falls

Zumwalt Meadow Loop, River Trails

Loop around Zumwalt Meadow is 1.5 miles round trip; to Roaring River Falls is 3.6 miles round trip

The hike around Zumwalt Meadow and along the South Fork of the Kings River shows off a gentler, more subtle side of Kings Canyon National Park—a contrast to steep Sierra slopes and towering sequoias.

Lawyer jokes aside, few attorneys are honored with their names attached to lovely landscapes. So it's with some surprise that we hikers learn that Zumwalt Meadow was named for Daniel K. Zumwalt, whose client was the Southern Pacific Railroad. History is hazy about Zumwalt's behind-the-scenes role in aiding the formation of General Grant National Park, forerunner of Kings Canyon.

Zumwalt Meadow, like its namesake's role in history, is fading away. Trees surrounding the meadow are slowly engulfing the grassy meadow, a natural progression that occurs frequently in the park and elsewhere in the High Sierra.

A second scenic attraction en route—Roaring River Falls—is also curiously named. The falls are named not for their roar but from the Roaring River that creates them. Some waterfall critics say the two falls (about 20 and 40 feet) resemble chutes more than cascades, though such distinctions seem irrelevant when eyeing the inspirational scene.

Sure you can visit Roaring River Falls by way of a paved, tourist-trafficked 0.2-mile path from Highway 180, but taking the long way via Zumwalt Meadow will add something very special to your park experience.

After your hike, walk the short path from road's end to Muir Rock. This rock outcropping by the Kings River was a favorite speaking platform of the great naturalist John Muir, who urged Sierra Club members and anyone else who would listen to preserve wondrous Kings Canyon.

DIRECTIONS: Follow Highway 180 nearly to its terminus at Roads End. Look for the signed parking area on the right side of the highway.

THE HIKE: Head down-river along the bank to a suspension bridge. Cross over the Kings River and head back up-river. Junction the loop trail and choose your route.

Fork right to begin a saunter along the south leg, which soon crosses a rock slide, boulders that rolled down from mighty Grand Sentinel towering to your right. Savor changing vistas of the river and meadow, as well as Grand Sentinel and North Dome.

The return (north) leg heads along the river with the meadow on your left this time. After joining a wooden walkway over a boggy area, you close the loop. Retrace your steps back to the suspension bridge and the parking lot or keep walking downriver from the suspension bridge another 1.8 miles to Roaring River Falls.

Oh chute! Roaring River Falls.

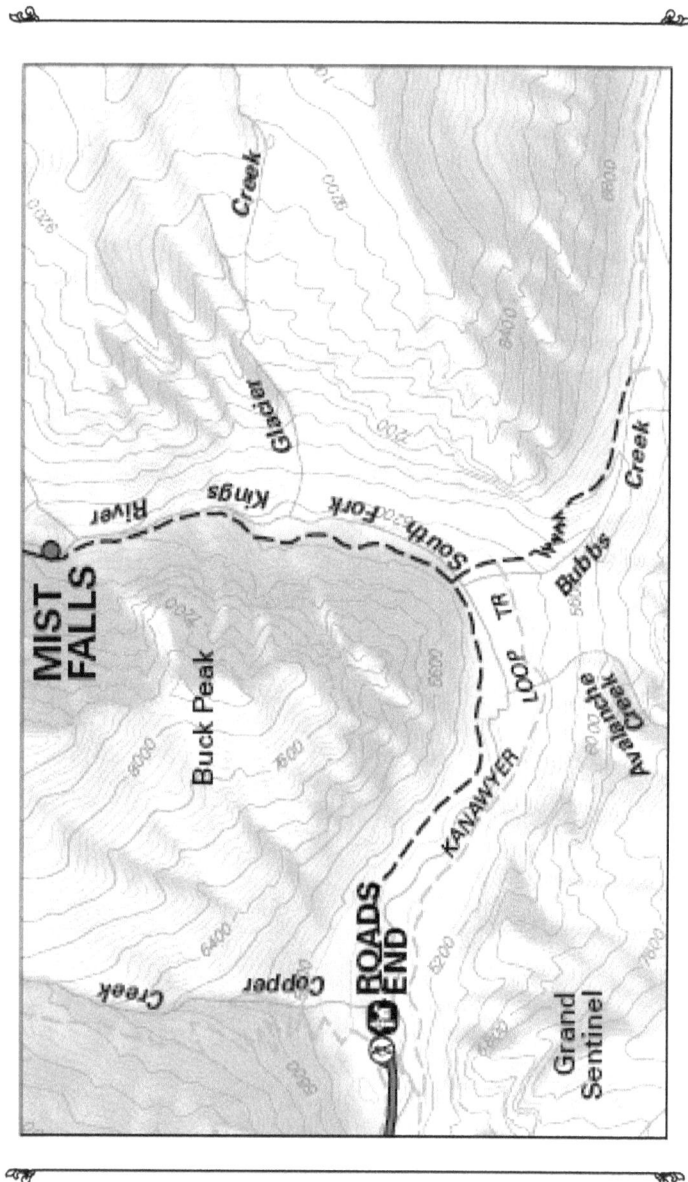

Mist Falls

Mist Falls Trail

8 miles round trip with 600-foot elevation gain

Six miles east of Cedar Grove Highway 180, the only highway in Kings Canyon National Park, comes to an abrupt end, its forward progress thwarted by towering and massive rock walls. But here at Road's End, trails begin.

One stellar trail is Mist Falls Trail, which leads hikers out of Kings Canyon and along the South Fork of the Kings River. Wind-whisked water from the cascades creates mist that keeps nearby environs forever cool and damp.

No waterfall connoisseur will mistake King Canyon's cascades for Yosemite's renowned falls, but some, like Mist Falls, are very special in their own way. Mist hovers around the lip of the falls and sprays the mossy rocks and trees down-river. Sometimes it's so misty, one can scarcely discern Mist Falls, which is not very high (50 feet or so) but puts on a great show.

Like other High Sierra waterfalls, Mist Falls is best in spring when the Kings River is at its most vigorous. Later in summer, the waterfall is considerably diminished.

The path is a busy one. In addition to the considerable allure of Mist Falls, the trail is attractive to hikers because there's not much pain or gain on this High Sierra hike; the 4-plus miles to the falls are fairly flat ones. Backpackers use this route on the way to Paradise Valley and Rae Lakes, as well as to jaunts on the John Muir Trail.

Well worth the hiker's consideration—coming or going—is the trail along Bubbs Creek, with deep pools that offer fishing and swimming (for those who like their water cold). The path travels below Avalanche Peak and crosses Avalanche Creek; note the many toppled trees—all pointing in the same direction—that suggest what prompted the "avalanche" place names.

The trail leads to the Bailey Bridge over the South Fork of the Kings River and connects to Mist Falls Trail. Combining the two trails makes an enjoyable 4.7-mile long loop and returning via Bubbs Creek adds 0.7 mile to the hike to Mist Falls.

DIRECTIONS: Take Highway 180 to the park's Big Stump entrance and Grant Grove. Proceed 37 winding miles to a parking lot and information station at Road's End, some 6 miles past Cedar Grove Village.

THE HIKE: Cross Copper Creek on a wooden footbridge and set out over flat, sunny terrain with a scattering of incense cedar and ponderosa pine. A mile and half out, the path leads into thicker, wetter, fern-filled forest.

At the two-mile (halfway) mark you reach a signed junction. The right fork leads over a bridge and along Bubbs Creek (see above). Stay left for Mist Falls.

Continue low along the canyon wall above the Kings River. The path heads north, passing through both thick, shady forest and exposed, open areas of brush and boulders.

Four miles out, the trail reaches an overlook above the falls. A short trail takes you down to the riverbank and base of the falls.

Dramatic views of Kings Canyon from the trails at this end of the park.

*Mighty Mt. Whitney:
A once-in-a-lifetime hike to be sure!*

EVERY TRAIL TELLS A STORY.

VII
MOUNT WHITNEY

HIKE ON.

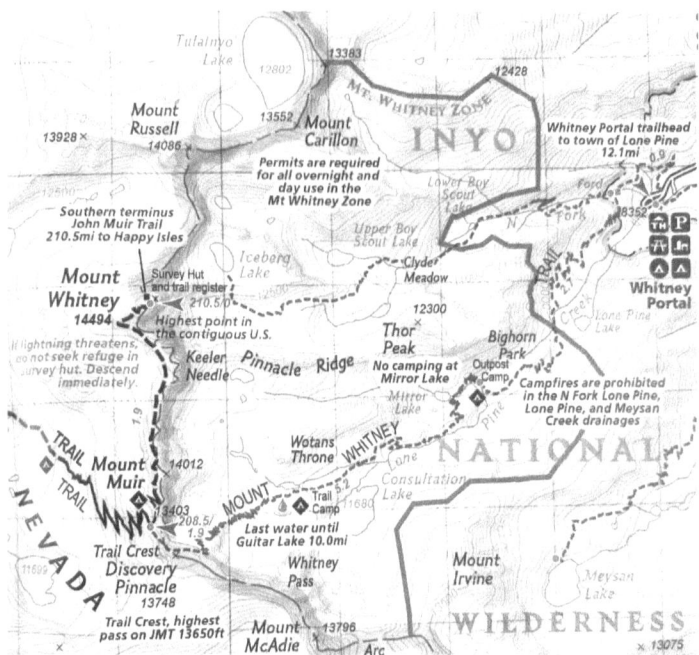

MT. WHITNEY

MT. WHITNEY TRAIL

From Whitney Portal to summit is 21.4 miles round trip with 6,100-foot elevation gain.

You can't get any higher than the 14,495-foot summit of Mt. Whitney, highest of all peaks in the continental U.S., and a once-in-a-lifetime (at least!) hiking experience. Hikers come from across the nation and around the world to climb Mt. Whitney Trail, which ascends the mountain's most accessible slopes.

The summit, on the eastern boundary of Sequoia National Park, can be climbed by the most fit and least altitude-sickness prone hikers in one day. Veteran hikers often make a before-dawn (3 to 4 a.m.) start for the climb to the peak.

You must secure a permit to hike to Mt. Whitney from the U.S. Forest Service, the agency administering the trail. The online Mt. Whitney lottery in February is the first opportunity to reserve a wilderness permit. Fastest way is to Google "Mt. Whitney permits" and navigate through the many details about the permit system on the Inyo National Forest site. For more info about the lottery and wilderness permits, call the U.S. Forest Service's Permit Reservation Office at 760-873-2483.

It's somewhat fitting, somewhat not, that this highest of the High Sierra was named for geologist Josiah Dwight Whitney. At Whitney's urging the California legislature founded and funded the California State Geological Survey in 1860 and placed him in charge.

In 1871, Whitney sent Clarence King, mountaineer extraordinaire and Geological Survey researcher, to the High Sierra for his second attempt (bad weather had hampered the first) at finding the highest peak. King reached what he thought was the highest peak and named it "Whitney." Alas, it was discovered a few years later that King had climbed the wrong peak (Mt. Langley) located 6 miles south.

Before King could return to scale the right peak, some Lone Pine residents climbed it and named it Fisherman's Peak.

The last couple miles of trail to Whitney's summit is the climax of the John Muir Trail, which begins in Yosemite Valley; this meeting on the map of Muir and Whitney is ironic because Whitney really disliked the great naturalist.

Mt. Whitney

Whitney had long insisted Yosemite Valley was the work of faulting. Upstart Muir advanced the then-revolutionary theory that Yosemite was carved by glaciers. "A mere sheepherder, an ignoramus," Whitney called Muir. "A more absurd theory was never advanced."

Unhappily for Whitney's place in geologic history, Muir's glaciation theory has proven to be largely correct. Still, Whitney's name remains at the top, elevation-wise anyway, a few hundred feet higher than 14,015-foot Mt. Muir, just south of Mt. Whitney.

Answering the call of science (astronomy, meteorology) and scientists, Lone Pine residents financed and constructed the Mt. Whitney Trail in 1904. In 1909 a stone summit hut (which still stands today) was built by the Smithsonian Institute to study Mars.

Over the years, the trail has been rehabilitated and realigned. It stands today—graded switchbacks hewn out of granite walls—as one of the finest examples in America of the trail-builder's art.

DIRECTIONS: From Highway 395 in Lone Pine, turn west on Whitney Portal Road and drive 12 miles to Whitney Portal.

THE HIKE: From Whitney Portal, the path ascends open country dotted with Jeffrey pine and white fir. About 0.75 mile out, a path forks west—the famed Mountaineer's Route used by climbers who tackle the eastern slope of the great mountain. Mt. Whitney Trail soon crosses the north fork of Lone Pine Creek and shortly thereafter enters the John Muir Wilderness.

Switchbacks, long and short, ascend nearly 2 miles over sun-drenched slopes to Lone Pine Lake,

The Trailbuilders Art at its finest: Whitney's switchbacks, shown here with prayer flags.

visible from the main trail. A short (200 yards or so) side trail leads to the rock-walled lake. Perfect for a (cold) swim.

After another half mile of climbing, the path skirts the south side of Bighorn Park (a long meadow), ascending alongside Long Pine Creek and, after crossing the creek, reaches Outpost Camp. It's a pleasant enough camp, but usually ignored by summit-bound hikers because it's too low and too far from the top.

Farther up the trail, 4.3 miles from the trailhead, is tiny Mirror Lake (10,640 feet). Switchbacking above the lake, the trail passes stunted foxtail pine and emerges above treeline. The path traverses Trailside Meadow, seasonally splashed with wildflowers. About 6.1 miles out, you climb to 12,000 feet and reach Trail Camp, last (highest) place to camp on the mountain.

Now tackle the famed switchbacks, 96 of them. First there are some longer ones and then, about halfway along the 2.25-mile ascent to Trailcrest, you'll encounter a series of switchbacks fitted with handrails. If you're hiking this trail when its icy, you'll know why the handrails were installed. Use them and appreciate them.

About 8.5 miles from the trailhead, reach Trailcrest, a pass located at 13,714 feet at the boundary of Sequoia National Park. With nearly a hundred switchbacks under your boots, you get a feeling of accomplishment when you look down at Trail Camp, seemingly so small and so far down the mountain.

The climb resumes as the path winds among large blocks of talus and between dramatic rock pinnacles. Enjoy stone-framed views of Owens Valley to the East. As for the western view, well, don't look if you're afraid of heights because there's quite a drop-off. Nevertheless, while an acrophobe's nightmare, the trail is plenty wide and distinct as it traverses the ridge.

About 10 miles out, Whitney's summit pops into view and you continue around to the southwest side

A high, High Sierra Pass! At Trail Crest, cross into Sequoia National Park.

of the peak. Choose among several steep summit routes marked with cairns. Gaining the summit, find a register next to the mountaineers hut, and the very highest point just east of the hut.

Oh, the view from all directions: To the north, the panorama of summits includes Mt. Williamson (second-highest peak in the continental U.S.) and to the south the procession of peaks includes Mt. Langley and Mt. Muir. To the west are the Sawtooth Peaks, the Kaweah Peaks and a section of the Great Western Divide and to the east, shimmering like some mirage far below is the Owens Valley.

While it's tempting to linger on the summit for a long and well-deserved rest, be aware that hikers frequently underestimate the length of time required for the descent. You do not want to rush down the mountain on rubbery legs—that's how injuries occur—and you want to return to the trailhead before dark. Enjoy your passage down the mountain but remember to stay focused and watch your step.

Remembered as the "Father of Sequoia National Park," newspaper editor George W. Stewart (R) led the campaign to establish the park. He wrote a book, "Big Trees of the Giant Forest," and the park's Mt. George Stewart (12,205 feet) honors him.

SEQUIOA AND KINGS CANYON STORIES

HIKE ON.

"The Sequoia and General Grant National Parks" by John Muir

from Muir's *Our National Parks*, published in 1901

The Big Tree (Sequoia gigantea) is Nature's forest masterpiece, and, so far as I know, the greatest of living things. It belongs to an ancient stock, as its remains in old rocks show, and has a strange air of other days about it, a thoroughbred look inherited from the long ago-the auld lang syne of trees. Once the genus was common, and with many species flourished in the now desolate Arctic regions, in the interior of North America, and in Europe, but in long, eventful wanderings from climate to climate only two species have survived the hardships they had to encounter, the gigantea and sempervirens, the former now restricted to the western slopes of the Sierra, the other to the Coast Mountains, and both to California, excepting a few groves of Redwood which extend into Oregon. The Pacific Coast in general is the paradise of conifers. Here nearly all of them are giants, and display a beauty and magnificence unknown elsewhere.

Except in picturesque old age, after being struck by lightning and broken by a thousand snowstorms, this regularity of form is one of the Big Tree's most distinguishing characteristics. Another is the simple sculptural beauty of the trunk and its great thickness as compared with its height and the width of the branches, many of them being from eight to ten feet in diameter at a height of two hundred feet from the ground, and seeming more like finely modeled and sculptured architectural columns than the stems of trees, while the great strong limbs are like rafters supporting the magnificent dome head.

The great age of these noble trees is even more wonderful than their huge size, standing bravely up, millennium in, millennium out, to all that fortune may bring them, triumphant over tempest and fire and time, fruitful and beautiful, giving food and

Muir's passionate writings convinced the powers that be to preserve (some) sequoia groves in national parks.

shelter to multitudes of small fleeting creatures dependent on their bounty.

Little is to be learned in confused, hurried tourist trips, spending only a poor noisy hour in a branded grove with a guide. You should go looking and listening alone on long walks through the wild forests and groves in all the seasons of the year.

In Nature's keeping they are safe, but through man's agency destruction is making rapid progress, while in the work of protection only a beginning has been made. The Mariposa Grove belongs to and is guarded by the State; the General Grant and Sequoia National Parks, established ten years ago, are efficiently guarded by a troop of cavalry under the direction of the Secretary of the Interior; so also are the small Tuolumne and Merced groves, which are included in the Yosemite National Park.

Far the largest and most important section of protected Big Trees is in the grand Sequoia National Park, now easily accessible by stage from Visalia. It contains seven townships and extends across the whole breadth of the magnificent Kaweah basin. But large as it is, it should be made much larger. Its natural eastern boundary is the high Sierra, and the northern and southern boundaries, and the Kings and Kern rivers, and thus including the sublime scenery on the headwaters of these rivers and perhaps nine tenths of all the Big Trees in existence. Private claims cut and blotch both of the Sequoia parks as well as all the best of the forests, every one of which the government should gradually extinguish by purchase, as it readily may, for none of these holdings are of much value to their owners. Thus as far as possible the grand blunder of selling would be corrected.

The value of these forests in storing and dispensing the bounty of the mountain clouds is infinitely greater than lumber or sheep. To the dwellers of the plain, dependent on irrigation, the Big Tree, leaving all its higher uses out of the count, is a tree of life, a never-failing spring, sending living water to the lowlands all through the hot, rainless summer. For every grove cut down a stream is dried up. Therefore, all California is crying, "Save the trees of the fountains," nor, judging by the signs of the times, it is likely that the cry will cease until the salvation of all that is left of Sequoia gigantea is sure.

"Frog Days in the High Sierra" by John McKinney
From New West Magazine, 1980.

Dave Bradford is becoming a mad scientist, or at least a madder one, as we splosh through this half-frozen High Sierra Meadow. We are up to our gaiters in a viscous mixture of mud and snow, stalking the wild Mountain Yellow-Legged Frog, the highest dwelling amphibian in the U.S. Our search is along the headwaters of the Kaweah River in Sequoia National Park has so far been in vain.

Bradford is upset because it looks like the previous brutal winter has done—in the entire population of *Rana muscosa*, the subject of his UCLA Ph.D. thesis. We've visited several unnamed lakes and found them still covered with ice. Bradford is worried about a frog kill, which, like a fish kill, occurs when lakes don't thaw and bacteria and fungi on the bottom consume all the oxygen.

We concentrate our efforts on a number of nameless football-field-sized lakes. (Larger lakes tend to have trout as well as names—the presence of fish being a strong incentive to man's naming proclivity—and trout tend to devour any Yellow Leg tadpoles that have the misfortune to be born in their vicinity.) It is on the banks of one of these unnamed lakes that we discover a grisly sight. Hundreds of yellow frog legs, minus their owners, are scattered about on shore. It looks like an amphibian version of the Donner Party.

"Blackbirds," Bradford mutters. He's seen such carnage before. As the tadpoles changed into froglets and hopped ashore, the birds pounced on them, eating everything but the nice, plump legs. Obviously not gourmets, these blackbirds.

Dispiritedly, we follow the Kaweah and ascend above timberline to a lush basin. Bradford changes into green sneakers, green shirt, green hat, green shades. The frogs must sense a kindred spirit because he immediately finds a Mountain Yellow Leg. It's a large female that he banded the previous summer. Bradford is delighted; after some 150 winter and summer days up here, he's become a bit unscientifically fond of the little buggers.

The Mountain Yellow Leg frog

The captured frog stoically endures the indignities of the tape measure, the scale and the rectal thermometer. Vital statistics: 68 millimeters from snout to rump; weight 27.3 grams; temperature, 22 degrees centigrade (a medium-warm frog). Stoicism, I soon learn, is what the MYL frog is all about.

Bradford goes about collecting tadpoles, leaving me to watch the female Yellow Leg and to guard his instruments from a marauding marmot. The frog moves but once in the next hour to snatch at a fly. She misses.

"Not too entertaining, are they?" teases Bradford, returning just as I'm picking up the frog to make sure it's still alive.

"It smells funny," I note.

"The frog secretes a mucous that doesn't taste good," he confirms. "Blackbirds and garter snakes like them, but they'll eat anything."

After 48 hours of observation, it is clear why no nature film crew has ever gone after the MYL. The lifestyle of this noxious-smelling creature seems deliberately un-dramatic. It hibernates seven to nine months a year in icebound ponds and is active (if you can call it that) for three to five months. After a night spent resting in the bottom of a lake or stream, it rises well after the sun and swims to shore. Here it makes its major decision of the day: where to bask in the sun. Once it finds a sunny spot, it moves only when the sun changes angle or to swallow flies. The MYL frog is known as a sit and wait predator and seems equally adept at both sitting and waiting. Gulping three flies in twelve hours is a good day's work. If the frog finds an especially nice, sunny spot, it may occupy the same square foot all day. Sometimes a Yellow Leg will join twenty or more of its fellows in a group bask, huddling in a heap, presumably to reduce heat loss.

Except for their communal basks, Yellow Legs are not sociable creatures. They croak only when stepped on, and it is a feeble call, more like a baby wrentit than a bullfrog. Courtship, carried on in the icy water, is a brief and desultory affair, but the sex act itself is prolonged and may go on for several days. The male, somewhat smaller than the female, hops on her back and with his special calloused thumbs, squeezes her behind the armpits. He massages out her eggs and fertilizes them in the water. The jelly-like eggs stick to aquatic vegetation, and the partners swim blithely off in opposite directions.

All in all, the MYL frog wants little more out of life than to stay warm; its ability to survive temperature extremes is what makes it an attractive research subject to Bradford. He implants transmitters in some of the frogs' bellies so that they give off a signal. The result is a series of beeps on an AM radio. So many beeps equal to so many degrees. The temperature readouts are quite accurate until a garter snake swallows the transmitting frog and becomes a transmitting snake. Snakes have completely different temperatures and can really screw up Bradford's data if he's not careful. To retrieve the expensive transmitter, Bradford must track down the snake and induce it to vomit, which comes naturally to the snake (it often vomits to offend predators or to lighten its load for a quick escape) but leaves everyone feeling a bit raw.

The MYL is a survivor. You have to respect this creature, whose chance for long life is as low as its metabolism. No other amphibian and few other life forms can withstand the extreme cold, the high elevation, the ruthless predators. Some of the frogs live to the ripe old age of 25, Bradford believes.

Although he conducts his research in one of the most beautiful alpine meadows on earth, there's little that is romantic or idyllic about his work. A campus flyer he circulated describing the delights of frog research failed to lure any pretty coeds into the Sierra. Bradford's nights are long and lonely. The silence is broken only by the radio, which receives but two transmissions: a rock station from Gilroy, and the endless beeping of his transmitting frogs.

Sequoia (NPS Pamphlet for Visitors, 1937)

Perhaps nowhere else is it possible to hike so easily for hours through such forests of sequoia, pine, and fir. Many of the trails are oiled to eliminate dust. The trail system is well signed, and the map in this pamphlet is used by many as a guide. It would be impossible to enumerate all the points of attraction or combination trips which can be made.

Alta Trail Nine miles from Giant Forest to Alta Peak (11,211 feet); passes through the Plateau of the Giant Trees and Panther, Mehrten, and Alta Meadows. The view from Alta Peak has been pronounced by members of the Sierra Club as fine as any in the California mountains.

Trail of the Sequoias Connects the High Sierra Trail from the saddle near Crescent Meadow, 3.7 miles to the Alta Trail, and passes through Big Tree groves rarely seen by the public before the opening of this trail.

Twin Lakes Trail From Lodgepole Camp, 5 miles to Clover Creek, and 2 miles farther to Twin Lakes, famous for unsurpassed scenic setting at 9,750 feet, and for good trout fishing. Above Twin Lakes on Silliman Shoulder is one of the finest panoramas of mountain scenery in the world.

High Sierra Trail This trail, one of the finest mountain routes in America, extends from the Big Trees of the Giant Forest to the summit of Mount Whitney (14,494 feet), highest mountain in continental United States. In Sequoia National Park the largest trees in the world are now linked by a splendid trail to the highest mountain peak in the country.

John Muir Trail This trail from Mount Whitney, in the Sequoia National Park, to the Yosemite Valley, in the Yosemite Park, is not clearly defined for all of the way on existing maps, but information concerning it may be secured by writing to the superintendent.

JOHN MCKINNEY

John McKinney is an award-winning writer, public speaker, and author of 30 hiking-themed books: inspiring narratives, top-selling guides, books for children.

John is particularly passionate about sharing the stories of California trails. He is the only one to have visited—and written about—all 280 California State Parks. John tells the story of his epic hike along the entire California coast in the critically acclaimed *Hiking on the Edge: Dreams, Schemes, and 1600 Miles on the California Coastal Trail.*

For 18 years John, aka The Trailmaster, wrote a weekly hiking column for the Los Angeles Times, and has hiked and enthusiastically told the story of more than 10 thousand miles of trail across California and around the world. His "Every Trail Tells a Story" series of guides highlight the very best hikes in California.

The intrepid Eagle Scout has written more than a thousand stories and opinion pieces about hiking, parklands, and our relationship with nature.

A passionate advocate for hiking and our need to reconnect with nature, John is a frequent public speaker, and shares his tales on radio, on video, and online.

JOHN MCKINNEY:
"EVERY TRAIL TELLS A STORY."

Hike On.

TheTrailmaster.com

www.ingramcontent.com/pod-product-compliance
Lightning Source LLC
Chambersburg PA
CBHW032041290426
44110CB00012B/908